beyond HEAD KNOWLEDGE

Pat and George
May you be blessed and
satisfied in H/M

In Christ
Naomi Sato
7/2/14

Beyond Head Knowledge

Knowing Christ Who Satisfies Our Hearts
© 2014 by Naomi Fata
All rights reserved

ISBN: 978-1-62020-268-5
eISBN: 978-1-62020-369-9

Cover Design & Typesetting by Hannah Nichols
eBook Conversion by Anna Riebe

AMBASSADOR INTERNATIONAL
Emerald House
427 Wade Hampton Blvd.
Greenville, SC 29609, USA
www.ambassador-international.com

AMBASSADOR BOOKS
The Mount
2 Woodstock Link
Belfast, BT6 8DD, Northern Ireland, UK
www.ambassador-international.com

The colophon is a trademark of Ambassador

beyond HEAD KNOWLEDGE

knowing *Christ*
who satisfies our hearts

Naomi Fata

AMBASSADOR INTERNATIONAL
GREENVILLE, SOUTH CAROLINA & BELFAST, NORTHERN IRELAND

www.ambassador-international.com

Endorsement

This book will absolutely change your perspective regarding what it means to know Christ and to walk with Him! As an autobiography, the author shares in a powerful and transparent way her personal journal from having only intellectual faith and Bible knowledge to developing a real, personal, growing relationship with God. In the pages of this book, she raises questions that many of us in the church often think about privately but are often hesitant to talk about. She also shows us—through her experiences and through the Scriptures—the life changing answers to those questions. The message of this book is a clarion call to believers to move past an intellectual, duty-based relationship with God to one of total trust, dependence, and intimate fellowship with Him.

~ Thaddeus Dragula, lead pastor,
First Baptist Church of Rhinebeck, NY

In memory of my father,
Barry C. Thorpe
1955-1991

Dedicated to my family, friends, and all who know me. My prayer is that they see evidence of my hope, not just in my written words but in my very life.

Contents

Acknowledgements

All glory goes to the Lord. The content of this book is only meaningful as I was taught by the Holy Spirit. I praise Him for the work He has done in my heart and thank Him for all of the amazing people He has put in my life to help me along the way.

For my husband, whose unfaltering faith in me has been a solid rock of support when I doubted myself.

For my mother, who diligently raised me to study and love the Word of God.

For Walter Irwin, who has been like a father to me for the past thirteen years, has mentored me, and counseled me through this entire book journey.

For John and Ellen Raimondo, whose love for the Lord helped to open the eyes of my heart.

For Joan Reynolds and Eleanor Seeland, who read through my manuscript and critiqued the content for sound biblical doctrine.

For Anna Ahrens and Karen Skinner, whose friendship has been steadfast through all the years.

Foreword

In science, a tropism is a growing toward a powerful drawing force. In spiritual matters, a hunger and thirst is the dynamic that draws us to our hope in God. Take away hope or expectancy in God's ability to show Himself to us, and we have an ineffective and powerless church.

This is the predicament that Naomi finds herself in as she takes us with her on a journey that ultimately reveals God's beauty and power to transform a life. A deep heart knowledge of God is the very essence of hope, and when hope has been born, there is an abiding confidence in all of the mighty promises.

A book for our time with a message for eternity; you will never be the same!

> *Broken and empty I stood*
> *To change my life if I could*
> *Tears of pain fall; He catches each one*
> *And dries my face with the warmth of His Son*
> *A whisper that His love will always abound*
> *A new person will awake from His hope I have found.*

Walter Irwin, Founder
www.christianresourceministry.com

Introduction

This book is one of self-examination and inner seeking, searching for the truths of the Bible to be evidenced in my life. Observing my own life and the lives of other Christians, I saw so little victory in Christ, deep inner joy, or peace that seemed to come from a supernatural source. I knew all these things were promised to us in Scripture but had to ask why they were not a reality in my own life. With all fervency I tried to follow God, but I could not seem to achieve the Christian life Christ spoke of in the Gospels.

In serving God I sensed Christian acts done out of deep brokenness instead of wholeness. At times I even wondered why I would want someone to become a Christian if there was no healing for our hearts until we get to heaven. As I examined my own faith, I became convinced that, true to His Word, God would heal brokenness and that I could live an abundant, joy-filled Christian life on earth.

Working with the general public for nearly ten years, I noticed the vast amounts of pain people carry around with them. In this sin-cursed world, life has become pain for Christians and non-Christians alike. But what about the freedom promised in Christ? Could this become a reality in all of our lives? Would not this be the greatest testimony of Christ's power on the earth? He could transform lives destroyed by the devil's work and fill us to overflowing with the glory of God.

All this I had studied until my head was filled with the knowledge of God and the Scripture but to no avail. My heart was still tormented by my own inner distress. Finally, when I came to Him knowing that only He alone could make me whole, the work of transformation began. From the depths of my heart, I began to know the power of God.

I believe that, no matter what has torn our hearts apart, there is healing in Christ; He is the answer to all of life's problems! When our hearts become filled with Him, His light shines, casting out our darkness.

Where are you in your Christian life? Are there questions buried in the crevices of your heart that have gone unasked? Do you find yourself quietly grasping for LIFE in the pages of your Bible, longing for living faith? If this is true of your life, I wrote for you—that you might know Him!

A hunger and thirst for God is the beginning of hope.

~ Walter Irwin[1]

---

1   http://christianresourceministry.com/2013/11/28/hunger-and-thirst-for-god/ used with permission

CHAPTER 1

A Saved Seeker

You will seek me and find me when you seek me with all
your heart.

~ Jeremiah 29:13

For as long as I can remember, I have longed for God and desired
to follow Him. I grew up in a Christian home; as the daughter of a
pastor, we were in church several times a week. Discussions about
God, the Bible, and theology were the norm of conversation around
the dinner table. At age four, through family devotions, my mother
spoke to me about accepting Christ into my life. I prayed, confessing
the sins of my young life, and received Him as my personal Savior.
From that time on I sought to follow Him with my whole heart.

I would estimate that before I was 20 years old, I had sat through
at least 1,040 sermons, and 5,400 evenings of family devotions. As
a teenager I read numerous books on prayer, holiness, and serving
God. I was devoted to Bible memorization and daily Bible reading.
After high school I even attended a year of Bible college. Looking
back, I know that it was a longing for God that compelled me to
seek Him. The diligence with which I read, prayed, and studied
was because I thought this was the avenue to knowing God. In

truth, it only amounted to a great deal of knowledge about God, doctrine, and the Bible.

While reading the Bible in my adolescence, several verses took root in my heart. Jeremiah 29:13 was one of them. For years it stirred in my soul. I wanted God. I was saved, but what did it mean to find God if I sought Him with my whole heart? I didn't want to settle for doing the Christian thing just because that's how I grew up. Since I received Christ as my Savior at such a young age, the fact that I was a sinner saved from eternal damnation and now bound for heaven became almost common place. But heaven bound didn't seem to be enough for me. If my salvation was only for heaven, what about hope for earth? Yes I had been saved, but I sensed that did not mean I had sought God with all my heart. What would I find in Him if I sought Him with my whole heart?

Deep down from somewhere inside of me, a nagging unrest about my soul told me something was amiss in my relationship with God. It wasn't that I was wandering away from God or that I had committed some great sins. Yet all the knowledge of God that I had gained still seemed to leave me with a sense of emptiness. As I went to church Sunday after Sunday, I would sit in the pew and sing the familiar hymns. Some were about victory in Jesus, having a river of life flowing out of me, power in the blood, and the greatness of God.

No Victory

The problem was I didn't sense any victory in Jesus. My life did not seem lived in victory. I felt nothing flowing out of me that would even vaguely resemble the flowing river of life that the song spoke of. Given that I was already saved, I believed that through the act of salvation, Christ had already manifested the power available to me through His blood. I could sing songs about God's greatness, but God seemed distant and far away. I knew that the Bible said He was great, and I could tell a person that God was great, but there was no emotion attached to it. The greatness of God was simply a fact to me, not something that would make my heart sing.

Also as I read the Bible, I noticed the zeal with which it was written; as the writers were inspired by God, they spoke of a God who was real to them. The words of the Bible spoke to me about a strong God, one who was powerful; a God who did things beyond what even my mind could conceive; a God whose love for me was so strong that even persecution could not separate me from a sense of His love; a God who parted the Red Sea; a God who led the wise men with a star; a God who was personal, real, and powerful. To me, God was confined to doctrine, theology, and prayer. Yet even in all this, I struggled to know how to pray or how to find God's will for my life. I often felt like the double-minded man in the Bible (James 1:6). My inner thoughts and emotions were always tossed about like waves on the open ocean.

Not only that, the apostles wrote of putting off the old man. I struggled to understand this, believing I had little of the old man to put off. If I had lived as a new creation since age four, how much could I possibly have to put off? Repeatedly the Bible mentioned joy and peace for believers. As I looked at my life, I did not observe true joy or peace coming out of my heart. I assumed that since the old man had been taken care of, I should automatically have the joy and peace the Bible talked about, but I could only do the Christian thing and fake joy so that others would think I was a great Christian. I could not fool myself.

I didn't have joy or peace. My soul did not feel filled with the light of God. I was frustrated. I didn't understand why. I tried to create peace but only felt turmoil. Admitting to such feelings would have caused me to feel guilty because it seemed so dishonoring to the God I was trying to love and serve. Therefore as best I could, I kept a cap on my struggles and tried to just continue on in doing the Christian things.

The Journey

By the time I was in my early twenties, I was so discontent with my faith—or lack thereof—that I began a journey. It has been a journey of seeking and searching and finding; of pounding on the doors of heaven with the promises of the Bible; of testing God because I could not believe; of inner searching to find the reason for my lack of joy and peace; and of finding the heartwrenching truth that even in all my righteous acts, I was a filthy sinner in need of forgiveness.

Now I stand on the other side of this journey, not as one who has finished the race but as one who has crossed over. What I found along the way was that all the years of struggle were due to a head filled with knowledge about God but a heart empty of knowing Him. The longing for Him was the longing of my heart to know Him. This might seem insignificant, but only when my heart knows Him can I begin to live in the fullness of all the Bible has for us as believers. When my heart knows Him I can fellowship with Him in a way no head knowledge can.

The Work of the Evil One

As I have grown and studied, I have become sharply aware of the fact that there is another party present in this journey. He is the evil one who has come to kill, steal, and destroy. If he can keep the knowledge of God out of my heart, he succeeds in his mission. Only by knowing God in my heart can I access the strength given by God to live this life. The evil one cares little if I study the Bible, go to church, and pray as long as it stays in my head. I am all for Bible reading, church, and prayer, but all that I learn must take root in my heart. The enemy of our souls is a master deceiver; he could not keep me from the Word, from church, or from doing what appeared to be Christian things, but he could carefully cloud my vision with a false perception of my relationship with God. He could attempt to keep the knowledge of God out of my heart, which would leave me helpless and wandering, empty inside.

Perhaps you wonder how it is that I know the distinction between head knowledge and heart knowledge. It would be a hard thing to explain. Very simply, little by little and sometimes a lot at a time, I began to feel the light of God bubbling up from deep within. The joy of fellowshipping with the God I love coming from the depth of my heart, overflowing, filling my life. Now I have a sure, unwavering confidence that God dwells on the inside of me. To me, I don't just know the Sunday school answer that when I accepted Christ as my Savior He came to live in my heart. I know so much more! I feel Him, feel the greatness of God filling the inner part of me.

As I thought about how to explain this, I thought about meeting my husband. At first when I met him, I slowly got to know little things about him that were mostly facts. These were facts like where he grew up, what year he graduated from high school, when his birthday was, where he lived, and a lot of other factual information about him. As our relationship grew, I began to learn more about what he thought and how he felt about different things. I observed his relationships with other friends to see whether he was kind and respectful. I could have transferred this into facts as well by simply saying that he is a kind, respectful young man who likes to spend time with those he loves. As a simple fact, this information would be true and could either remain as head knowledge about him or could stir my heart to begin to love him. I used these facts about him to teach my heart to know his character, which is what caused me to marry him. All the factual information was very helpful in guiding my heart and kept me from foolishly marrying a mean man. I remember times, even after engagement when I was in love with him, that I would check the facts to make sure the love I felt in my heart was not leading me astray. As all the facts about him were cultivated in my heart, I fell in love with him in a way my head could not. Deep love flows up from the heart, not from the head.

The Bible is filled with facts and real life examples about God. Just reading them gave me a lot of facts about God, but I had to get past the factual stage of the relationship or else it would remain an almost meaningless relationship. What I noticed was that even though I spent much time doing things that were about God—like Bible reading, prayer, and memorization—I was only learning factual information. All the facts needed to become meaningful and engrain themselves in my heart so that I could truly know Him.

Eight years ago if you had asked me if I knew God, truly knew Him in my heart, I am sure that I would have answered rather defensively. I would have told you that of course I know God. After all, I had been a Christian for nearly two decades and had never fallen into any deep sin. My main desire was to serve God and be a good testimony. How could anyone possibly think that I did not know God in my heart? The truth is probably very few people had any inkling that I did not. Even though I would try my best to convince you that I knew God in my heart, I know that the question would have stayed with me. I would have wrestled with it, wondering if I really did know Him.

My Former Self

Looking back, I hardly recognize who I once was. Not much in my outer circumstances may have changed. I still live in the same general area, still know the same people, and have followed the somewhat normal trend of growing up, getting married, and having children. Recently I had a rather disturbing encounter with a situation and person in which I saw a mirror image of my former self. Through this incident I was brusquely reminded of exactly how dark life was without the heart knowledge of God. When only my head knew about God, I had been a twisted, tangled mess of doctrine, fear, judgmental attitudes, and so much more. I can hardly explain the inner turmoil that raged inside as I tried to force myself to live according to the Bible yet felt tossed about by my human effort. Head knowledge caused me to be harsh and religious, insecure and angry. Heart knowledge floods over all these, giving me an overwhelming sense of God's love.

As I reflected on this encounter, I found myself quite unable to put this change in my heart into words. The Lord led me to begin to write down my journey, and so this book was born. Very simply, it is a testimony of my faith. Through it I will endeavor to write about how I worked through strongholds, recognized roots of sin, began to truly trust God, learned how to fight against my flesh, and gained a greater understanding of my calling. I have found that it is not my efforts to please God that transformed my life but instead having an intimate relationship with the One who is good, holy, true, compassionate, and filled with love. Only through the revelation of the Holy Spirit of God did all this come to pass.

Sweet Fellowship

What I have found through my journey is that when the knowledge of God so fills my heart, I begin to enjoy sweet fellowship with Him. It isn't about how much I can do for Him (pray, memorize, or study) but about knowing Him. As I know Him, He brings Scripture to life. I begin to know Him in my inner being. My heart communes with Him. His love floods over me and fills my empty places. He captivates my heart, causing Him to be the focus of my desires. It becomes almost easy to battle strongholds of fear, judgment, shame, guilt, and insecurity when my heart knows Him.

This is what I was saved from: lack of fellowship. At the cross where Jesus died, He paid the price so that I might be close to God. The gap of sin that separated me from Him was closed. If you have heard this all your life like I had, please do not let the power of it pass you by. It isn't just so that I would be saved from eternal separation from God. It is also for the now; to know God now while I live on this earth; to enjoy the same fellowship with Him that Adam and Eve had in the garden before they sinned. I want to walk and talk with God now in this life.

As I sought Him with all my heart I found a fellowship deeper than I had ever known—the knowing of Him deep in my heart. Through knowing Him, the revelation of what I have been saved from began to dawn on me. Yes, I was saved and heaven bound, but still lived in bondage. I lived my Christian life as if it were a religion. Now as I have come out of bondage and my heart is filled with His love, the pretense of religion fades into history. Until my heart knew His love, until my heart knew fellowship with Him, I did not know what I was missing. The Bible is so true in saying that the joy and peace that comes from knowing God can be found only in Him!

I commenced my seeking with an unrecognizable longing in my heart. All I knew was that I was in pursuit of God. Possibly the simplest way to communicate the difference between knowing God in one's heart versus one's head is to share my story. As the hope that I have found in Christ rises to fill my heart, I have been compelled to share because I believe many other Christians have this longing to know God. There is always room for growth in each of our Christian lives. None of us will fully know Him on this side of heaven. While on earth we see as though looking through a glass or a mirror, we have a reflection of who He is; but one day when we all get to heaven, we will see Him face to face.[2] Even in my

---

2   1 Corinthians 13:12

marriage I do not fully know my husband, but with each passing year, I can know and love him more.

The good news is that even though we will not fully know God while we are on earth, He has given us the Holy Spirit to live in us. He will teach us about the Father, and our hearts can begin to know Him here on this planet.

Life Application Questions

1. Have you accepted Christ as your personal Savior? If you have not, please do so. Confessing your sins and receiving Him into your life as your Savior and Lord is the first step to knowing God. Take this first step by saying a prayer. You don't have to use a lot of words. Even if you are unsure of what to say, He knows your heart.

2. Write or think about your testimony, which would include your salvation experience and any work that God has done in you to transform your life as you have grown in your walk with Him.

3. Ask God to examine your heart. Judge your life by the fruit you experience (Luke 6:44). Do you see the fruit of the Spirit according to Galatians 5:22–23?

4. Write a prayer thanking God for your faith in Him and asking that He would continually open your heart to know Him in a deeper way.

CHAPTER 2

Feelings of Darkness

If I say, "Surely the darkness will hide me and the light
become night around me," even the darkness will not be
dark to you; the night will shine like the day, for darkness
is as light to you.

~ Psalm 139:11–12

Jarred awake by the sound of a child crying in the next room, I
opened my eyes to darkness. The power must have gone out some-
time during the night so even the nightlights were out. Carefully I
made my way to the child's bedroom, groping along the furniture
to find the way. Surrounded by the familiarity of my own home,
I had a good sense of direction even in the dark. My first thought
was to look for a flashlight, but my eyes quickly adjusted to the
darkness, so I disregarded thought of light. I had become accustomed to the darkness.

How true this is of our spiritual lives as well. Rather than
seeking the full light of the Bible, often we settle for darkness
because we get accustomed to being surrounded by it. The words

of Scripture that promise our hearts light are left forgotten as we stumble through life.

In a rather inexplicable way, I felt a dark cloud surrounding my life, confused about my directions, sensing God was distant and far off. Deep inside I questioned if God was even on my side, because so often everything I thought I would do for Him did not come to pass. At times I even sensed that perhaps He was purposefully blocking my way. In all my good Christian acts of Bible reading, Scripture memory, and the desire to please God, I still felt a deep darkness surrounding my very soul.

Early on in my life, as early as grade school, I recall attempting to witness to people or trying to get them to understand that the Bible was real. Nearly every time, I entered into these discussions with theological arguments and reasoning, trying to question people out of their own belief, as if getting them to see that their views were wrong would change their life. My discussions were all concentrated on intellectually convincing people that Jesus is the way.

While in high school I always viewed myself as one who lived for God. I had my hopes and dreams ahead of me, and they were all centered on serving God—going to the mission field and Bible college. It was almost as if I used my focus to be a witness for me, thinking that the direction of my life toward Christian service automatically made my Christian witness successful.

Secular Workplace

During my senior year of high school, I entered the secular workplace. I continued to try to use my directions and dreams of what I planned to do for God as part of my witness. This served to keep the spotlight off any underlying turmoil or questions that were buried in my heart. Even though I was not even sure if God was on my side, because so often I felt that I was running into obstacles that He had placed in my path, I still wanted to be a good testimony for Him.

As I worked in the world, I knew the concept that I was supposed to be salt and light, but slowly I became aware that I didn't feel like I was shining any light in my workplace. Sometimes I would catch my thoughts mirroring the attitudes of my non-Christian coworkers: frustration with life and living; anger with myself, my circumstances, and my life. A frequent phrase that I heard coworkers say was "I can't take it anymore." I felt the same way but wondered what it was that we "couldn't take anymore." Quite literally I think all the pressures of life seemed to be pressing in, and it seemed too great a burden to bear; everything from financial pressure to struggles in relationships creates stress in our lives whether we are Christians or not. I knew in my head that I was supposed to be giving all my stress to Christ and that Christ was supposed to be the answer to all my problems, so I would try all the harder to conquer this negativity that I felt welling up inside me. As I tried to witness, I often found myself wondering what I was really offering the unsaved. I wondered why, if I as a Christian who was supposedly filled with the power of God, "couldn't take it anymore," and couldn't deal with the problems of life in general, why would the non-Christian world want what I have?

My coworkers were from a variety of backgrounds: some devout Muslims, others attended the Unification Church seminary, and others were from mainline liturgical denominations. (I do not pretend to know if those in the more Bible-based denominations were saved or not, but from outward appearances and conversations I would think that they were not.) All these people knew that I went to church and was a strong moral person with a devout belief in God. We would talk about our faith frequently.

While in Bible college, which I attended a year after high school, I had studied these different religions and had a basic understanding of their belief systems. I had always been taught and believed that the foundation of my Christian faith was that I worshipped a resurrected living Savior and had a personal relationship with the living Son of God. As I conversed with these coworkers about their faiths, I realized that they were very earnest in what they believed as well. I wondered what it was that caused them to believe so sincerely in their faith, when mine was obviously (to me) the right one. As I began to question, I had this growing sense that this "faith" or "belief system" that I had formed as a Christian did not seem as alive as I had been taught. My personal relationship with Jesus that I was trying to convince others of did not seem that personal. The problem was I didn't feel like it was a personal relationship. In fact, I didn't feel like it was a relationship at all. I am in no way saying that we should live our Christian lives by feelings, but the Bible does teach that we have the power and presence of God in us. As this gnawing questioning continued, I began to wonder if I was just trying to follow a religion like those who followed other religions. They were faithful in prayer; so was I. They were faithful in reading their Scriptures and doctrine; so was I. They knew how to share their faith; so did I. The Bible said I had the truth, that Jesus is the way. My "religion" or "faith" was not the living faith of Scripture, and I knew it.

Faithfully day in and day out, I read the Bible. I read about the fruits of the Spirit: love, joy, peace, patience, goodness, and faithfulness (Galatians 5:22). I had heard so many teachings about this, about how as a Christian we have these fruits and just have to exercise them. I tried to follow the principles of all this teaching. I tried to have peace, joy, and love. I tried and tried, as if the human effort would produce them. I had no joy and no peace, which the Bible said I was supposed to have. Often I felt tormented by guilt and shame because I was not producing the fruit of the Spirit. I could pretend on the outside, but I knew I did not have true joy or peace in my heart. Now I know these fruits are only manifested in my life through the work of the Holy Spirit. I cannot generate them by human effort but can cooperate and obey the Spirit to produce them in me.

Direction from God

I diligently prayed about God's will for my life, that He would show me the way to go, that He would open the doors. I knew I wasn't praying with faith. I had too many doubts bubbling up in my mind. James 1:6–8 says that when we pray, we should have faith and not doubts, because doubting tosses us about like the waves of the ocean. If we pray with doubt, we cannot expect to receive from the Lord. I felt like this double-minded man in this passage. I knew I was seeking God's will with a lot of doubt, but I didn't know how to believe. Not only did I not know how to believe, but also I didn't know what was God's leading and what was not. One minute I would think He was leading me in one direction, and the next minute I would toss that out to think He was leading me in another direction. My soul was not at peace with anything. Sometimes when I prayed, I would get a temporary peace that would last a couple days or a week, but then I would feel something else creep in. I didn't know what this something else was, but now as I look back I would categorize it as bondage. Everything I prayed about, I felt like I prayed with doubt. I was angry with myself for doubting, frustrated that I couldn't believe, but I didn't know how to stop doubting. My soul was in such unrest that I could not sense the still small voice of God.

Repeatedly over the course of my teen years and young adult-hood, I had publicly gone forward at altar calls, dedicating my life to service to the Lord. In private I repeatedly did the same. I had this unquenchable desire to serve God, but I couldn't feel Him; I couldn't sense any direction. At eight, I went forward at summer camp to commit my life to Christian service. From this time on when people asked what I wanted to be, I said "a missionary." At twelve, I signed a purity vow that I would stay sexually pure until marriage. At thirteen, I went forward at a Word of Life snow camp and signed a commitment dedicating all of my days to God, which also in my mind was a renewal of my dedication to mission work, telling God once again that I would go anywhere in the world for Him. (This signed commitment is still in my Bible today.) At fourteen, I remember making a private decision to read the Bible through in one year, and I completed this goal in half a year. At sixteen while on mission trip, I made another commitment to Christian service. At eighteen, I went forward in church to dedicate my life to service.

From early adolescence, I filled my life with reading all sorts of books on purity, holiness, and prayer. I faithfully had a quiet time with God every day from early childhood on. The days that I didn't, I felt guilty. I had been given the advice to write "God wasn't worth it to me today" on the days that I didn't do my devotions so that I would feel remorseful. I did this too and, yes, I felt remorseful. I kept trying to give God my all, but I felt like He wasn't using all this commitment for anything. This added to my mounting inner frustration and anger.

Inner Turmoil

As I was beginning to write about this portion of my life, I flipped through my Bible and found numerous verses underlined and dated, most of them reflecting my inner darkness. One that stands out among the others is Job 3:26 where Job wrote that he had no peace or rest but only turmoil. This was exactly what I was feeling—turmoil. I have already expressed that I felt angry and frustrated, but at the time I did not even know that was what I was feeling. As I said previously, I was completely out of touch with what I was feeling. All I knew was that I had deep inner turmoil.

I also re-read some of the poems that I wrote at that time. All of them had the haunting fear of failing God. My desire was to serve Him, but I was terrified of living a worthless life. I lived afraid that each step might not "be God's will." It was like I expected God to open up heaven and write in bold words across the sky exactly what I was supposed to do or where I was supposed to serve. I was seeking God but was unacquainted with the way in which He leads His children. While my soul was in such inner turmoil, I would believe for a moment that He called me to do a thing and then turn back because my soul did not seem at peace. The simple truth was that my soul was never at peace with anything. I had too many conflicting emotions raging inside to have any sense of peace. The following is one of the poems I wrote that so clearly reflects the inner battle inside me.

Constant fear
That I might not
Do Your will –
Will I fail?
And what if
These plans fall
Into pieces
Does that mean
I've failed You?

How often
I forget
The world is
In Your hand
You are still
On the throne
Yes, evil may
Befall me –

Only if
You let it
Yes, my plans
May change
Only if
You let them

For me I
Must follow
Though I only
See through the
Glass dimly
I must just
Seek You and
Follow You
You'll take care
Of the rest

Woven throughout the poem is biblical truth that God is in control and that I must follow Him, but also entangled in the biblical truth is my skewed sense of God and my relationship with Him. Even in this poem I was trying to convince myself that it was okay for me to change directions all the time because I was seeking Him, and I thought maybe God was just testing me to see if I would do anything He asked. All through the Bible it talks about "following God." I thought the following meant more Bible reading, more prayer. I was devoted to all of this, so I assumed that I must be following Him even if I had no peace and felt like I was always changing my mind. In the previous chapter, I briefly described some of the times I began to do something and changed my mind: applying to a new college, applying to be a missionary. This pattern was far reaching into every area of my life, so much so that I never did anything because after I would start, I would stop soon after because I wasn't sure it was God's will. This left me paralyzed by indecision, which only added to the mountain of inner turmoil.

Pondering the Lives of Others

During the months and years following my time at college, I spent many hours jogging. Somehow it was a way to let all this turmoil out. I would pray and talk to God, even though I felt like God was far away and that my prayers never went higher than the trees; yet I still sought Him and His presence. One jog in particular is very clear in my mind. That day I was discouraged and felt like life wasn't going anywhere. Over the course of my Christian life, I loved to read biographies. I had read about Keith Green, a Christian songwriter; Joni Eareckson Tada, a handicapped woman who used her life for the glory of God; David Livingston, a missionary to Africa; George Mueller, a man of faith who founded many orphanages; Amy Carmichael, a missionary to India; and so many more. I wanted to be like them, to leave a legacy of faith and courage so that God could be glorified. I remember these thoughts circling in my mind, "How is it that these people were used of God? How is it that He used them for so much? What if I don't make it? What if I don't fulfill my calling? What then? Will I have failed God? How can I make sure that I don't fail? What does it mean to follow God? I'm trying so hard, I will go anywhere He wants—Africa, Papua New Guinea, Quebec, anywhere. I don't care if there are no amenities of life, I don't care if it is halfway around the world, but why doesn't He show me where?" More than anything I didn't want to reach the end of my life to look back filled with regret that I didn't give God my all. I wanted my life to count for something, to be lived for God.

I had also been reading a book that contained a story that gripped my heart. It was about an invalid woman lying in the hospital. Her life did not consist of much, and she had no hope of recovery. Someone asked her what she thought about as she lay in her bed every day, and her reply was that she thought about Jesus and how good He was to her.[3] I didn't get it! Why was she able to think about how good Jesus was to her, and I couldn't? I had so much more in life than she had, but I couldn't think about Jesus and how good He was to me. I knew that if I had to lie in bed every day with no hope of recovery, I would most certainly not have that kind of peace and joy flowing out of me. I had two legs, two feet, a job, and things to do, yet I didn't have peace. When I thought about Jesus, I didn't have any feelings of goodness. What was wrong with me? I was trying to serve Jesus with my life, completely committed to going anywhere in the world He wanted me to go, but I didn't know Jesus like this woman did. Why? Why? Why? This seemed to be my neverending question.

Hidden Heart Issues

You might be wondering why I never asked anyone these questions. Probably there are many reasons. To begin with, I thought people viewed me as a "good" Christian girl, so how could I ask questions? My "good Christian" image might be tainted if I asked questions. Perhaps I was too proud to ask. Seventeen years of Christian learning told me that I had the answers. I knew the Bible and had much Scripture memorized, so I tried to hide my questions underneath my head knowledge.

Deeper than this were issues of my heart that taught me to be the chameleon—to hide in the shadows so that I wouldn't be noticed. I remember being in school, trying to be as quiet as possible so the teacher wouldn't call on me, not because I didn't know the answer but because I didn't want the attention. Hardly ever

---

3   Ortberg, John. (1997) *The Life You've Always Wanted.* Grand Rapids, MI. Zondervan Publishing House, 24–29.

did I ask questions in a group setting. I was too insecure; asking questions meant being vulnerable.

All this meant that I had many unhealthy relationships. I was afraid of vulnerability and had few close friends. Fear of authority figures at church and school plagued my heart. The dread that someone would get close enough to see the tangled mess inside caused me to keep people at a distance. I was friendly but afraid of deep relationships in which I would have to share the true me.

Only now can I look back and recognize my heart issues. At the time I was completely disconnected from what was in my heart and saw only what was on the surface. From the exterior all I noticed was this vague feeling that I was not who I should be in Christ, that there should be more to my faith than I was living out. I knew that the overflow of my heart was not what Scripture told me I should have.

I could have stopped searching, choosing to blame my darkness on childhood, circumstances in my life, pain from my father's early death, or any other unpleasant thing that happened to me. From reading Scripture I knew in my head that the world is sinful and that sin brings pain. Yet I also knew that Jesus died to take away my sin, gave me a clean heart, and promised me an abundant life of joy and peace in my heart. I thank God that He gave me the grace to continue seeking Him rather than becoming disillusioned and turning to the world. Thankfully I never did seek to find answers anywhere else. He gave me enough head knowledge to know that the Bible was the answer.

The Blessing of a Mentor

Through my job at a local convenience store, I met two people who have had a profound effect on my life since then. I believe God in His infinite wisdom purposefully brought these two people into my life.

The first person I mention is a local locksmith, Walt, who has been serving our community for many years. He is no ordinary locksmith; his work is simply a means of loving people to Christ and encouraging the local body of believers. To Walt, his job as a locksmith is the mission field God has called him to. Many years ago he was led to start Christian Resource Ministry, which is not an organization, but merely the vision that laypeople glorify God with their work. The foundational principle of Christian Resource Ministry is that each Christian layperson is a resource for the Lord. The functional aspect of exactly what each person does for a living is not nearly as important as whether each day is lived with the focus on serving Christ and fellowshipping with Him.

One day Walt came into my workplace to purchase some gas. Being the outgoing Christian that he is, he saw my nametag and immediately started a conversation with me about my name being from the Bible. Through this conversation, Walt found out that I was a Christian as well. From then on when he was in the area, he would stop by my workplace to encourage me with a Scripture or a little article from a Christian magazine.

Slowly over the course of several years, I began to share my poetry with Walt. I had come to a point of trusting him not to judge my questions. Even though I did not directly ask him most of the questions that were tumbling around inside of me, through my writing he got the sense that I was deeply seeking God but was struggling with my faith. I wrote as one who, though saved, had an empty ache in my soul that could only be filled by God.

The articles that Walt gave me challenged my thinking about God and the box that I had put Him in. One article in particular that I remember had to do with God's will. This issue was one of enormous concern to me. Throughout my life I felt tormented by fear of whether I was following God's will. At every new opportunity, I hesitated to move forward because I was terrified that

I might not be doing God's will. The article pointed out that part of God's direct will for our lives begins with simply living a godly life, being kind, gentle, loving, and doing those specific commands that are in Scripture such as love your neighbor as yourself, help the poor, honor your parents, walk in love, etc. The information in the article was nothing new to me. It contained the same truths of Scripture that I had heard hundreds of times from church and my own personal Bible reading. Somehow it caught my attention enough for me to realize that I was too focused on what great thing I was going to do for God and not enough on living my Christianity in my present situation. One day at a time, I could concentrate on doing the direct will of God.

In a very kind sort of way, Walt was telling me, "How can you expect to be a missionary in a foreign land if you don't care about the hurting people surrounding you every day?" This was a wakeup call. It helped me stop focusing so much on what I would be in the future and begin to focus a little more on being used of God in my current situation. As I began to reach outside myself and stop always thinking that I needed to know exactly what big thing God wanted me to do in life, I was able to lighten up a little. My approach to each day became a little more joyful as I asked God to use me in my day-to-day activities of work.

Working in a convenience store, I encountered hundreds of people a day; the Lord began to open my eyes to how much pain these ordinary people carry around with them every day. God challenged me to tell them I would pray for them, write them a card, or just genuinely listen to them. To me all this seemed like "not doing enough for God," but slowly I began to understand that Jesus was very interested in people. He loved people, and He called me to do the same. I had always believed that Jesus loved people, but I thought that meant witnessing and leading people to Christ, so I struggled deeply with the simplicity of being a loving person to the unsaved world, caring about their needs. I began to realize human pain. Broken people surrounded me, people struggling from the pain of divorce, death of a family member, news of a deadly illness, loss of work, eviction, household abuse, and innumerable other painful situations. Looking back, I notice that I had been calloused to the pain of others partly because I was out of touch with my own pain. While my own heart was living in brokenness, it was difficult to sense the pain of others, therefore making my efforts of Christian compassion stiff and almost unfeeling. One of the most important lessons I learned during this season was to truly love others, to listen to their needs and not jump to preach to them.

One verse that Walt shared with me changed the course of my thinking. In John 10:10, Jesus says that He came so that we might have life to the full. Walt seemed so joyful about this life that we might have to the full. It made me angry and frustrated inside. What full life? What was in that verse that anyone could be excited about? Why was I not excited about it? What was wrong with me? This questioning caused me to think. More than thinking, it was that I wrestled with the concept of an abundant life. I had always chosen to believe that this "abundant life" or "full life" meant my eternal life in heaven. In fact, I think I thought every promise in the Bible was intended only for heaven, which is why I failed to understand the value of my faith here on earth. If someone had asked me if I had abundant life, I'm sure I would have said yes because I thought I did—eternal life in heaven. As I contemplated all this, my anger grew because I couldn't understand what it had to do with the present. How was I supposed to live the next eighty years of my life looking forward to an abundant life in heaven? Is the promise of that abundant life in heaven enough to cause me to live for Christ today? The thought of living the rest of my days on earth only looking forward to "abundant life" in heaven was more revolting to me than it was appealing. My journey became one of trying to understand the concept of what is the fullness of life Jesus promises us here on earth.

Another Scripture that Walt shared with me was Mark 9. In this passage, Jesus is working with a demon-possessed boy. He tells the father that anything is possible for those who believe. In verse 24, the father responds confirming that he does believe—but immediately adds a prayer that Jesus would help his unbelief. This struck yet another chord with me. I grappled with this issue of believing: trying to believe but feeling no faith, like the one in James chapter one, always tossed about by doubt. I knew this was not strong, vibrant faith in the Son of the Living God.

Meeting my Future Husband

The second important person I met through my job at the convenience store is now my husband, Tony. When I first started working at the store, Tony had asked me if I had a boyfriend, and I said no. For the next several years, Tony continued to be a regular customer in the store. I had moved from being the front counter clerk to managing the one-person deli that was also in the store. Tony became a daily customer for breakfast and lunch. Often he would bring me new recipes to try and would stop to chat a little. Sometimes he would talk to me about his Christian life and the things he was involved in with his church, helping with the homeless ministry and sharing the gospel on the streets of a nearby city. He talked about God with this childlike faith, uninhibited by the darkness that I felt in my Christian life. It seemed like he grasped the truths of the Bible far better than I did. Frequently I would hear Tony say, "God is good." He said it as though he meant it and believed it. Although Tony was a much newer Christian than I and had much less Bible knowledge, he had an unwavering confidence in the character of God that flowed out from his heart. This far outweighed my head knowledge of any theology about the goodness of God; even more than that, I could sense true joy radiating out of Him when he talked about God. God was real to him.

I was drawn to this faith that Tony had. Shortly afterward, we began our courtship, but even more importantly, it was the beginning of a journey for me. It was the journey of my heart as I began to uncover the lies I had allowed into my heart and the deep issues that had taken root in my heart that kept me from truly knowing God. It was a journey that led me to a deep, heartfelt faith in the God of the Bible, the kind of faith I so much admired in Tony.

Life Application Questions

1. Do you feel any spiritual sense of emptiness or darkness?
2. Do you think that your faith in Christ is alive, and that the living aspect of your faith makes it different from that of people who follow other religions?
3. Think about the goodness of God.
4. Do you find yourself vacillating about God's will for your life? Are you confused about His will in general? Write down any specific directions in Scripture that point to God's will for all Christians.
5. Write a prayer or poem to God about any feelings of darkness that you have and any questions you have that may have formed from reading this chapter.

CHAPTER 3

His Touch on My Heart

I pray that your hearts will be flooded with light so that you can understand the confident hope he has given to those He called-his holy people who are his rich and glorious inheritance. I also pray that you will understand the incredible greatness of God's power for us who believe Him. This is the same mighty power that raised Christ from the dead and seated Him in the place of honor at God's right hand in the heavenly realms.

~ Ephesians 1:18–20, NLT

A bride walks up the aisle to melodious music, takes the hand of her fiancé, and anticipates the moment when the reverend pronounces them man and wife and bestows permission to kiss the bride. She longs for the touch of her groom on her lips. As the bride of Christ, do we long for the embrace of our Beloved?

Shortly before I started my relationship with Tony, Walt shared Ephesians 1:18–20 with me. He talked about these verses with excitement over what God has available for believers during this life. This passage was not new to me, so I struggled to comprehend what he was so excited about. I began to read these verses over and over, searching for something deeper than just words on a page. For weeks I searched for the source of Walt's enthusiasm. It stirred my soul yet frustrated me at the same time. Always before, I had viewed it in terms of my eternal life in heaven: I would be surrounded by His light in heaven and in heaven I would experience the greatness of God. I tried to tear the verses apart with Bible study about the words and cross reference other Scripture, but it did not help me grasp anything that Paul was talking about here. Through this I did realize that most definitely these verses were intended for life on earth, not heaven. Yet I knew my heart was not flooded with light. I did not understand any glorious riches. Most certainly I did not know any power in my relationship with Christ.

Finally, I grasped that Paul was praying this as a prayer for the church in Ephesus. I figured that if Paul could pray it for someone else, I should be able to pray it for me. For weeks, maybe months, I prayed these verses as a prayer, asking that God would flood my heart with light and show me the hope He has, asking that I would understand the greatness of His power. I did not receive an answer right away, but I kept persisting because the fervency with which Paul wrote these verses had rooted into my soul. I wanted what was available to me in this life through Christ. I didn't want to live the rest of my days without having a heart filled with the light of God.

In the meantime, as I was struggling in prayer to understand these verses, I was also beginning a courtship with Tony. Early in our relationship, I began visiting the church he attended. At the time there were a lot of messages about the heart: how Jesus had come to bind up the broken hearted, set the captives free, and release the prisoners from darkness (Isaiah 61:1). I had never considered the fact that Jesus came to release me from darkness, but I did know I had an awful lot of darkness. Like long buried hope aroused, my heart stirred with the hope that maybe this was the path to abundant life in Christ. I began to feel that perhaps I was broken hearted. I didn't know why. I had always convinced myself that everything was okay.

When I went out jogging, I began to dwell on this verse in Isaiah and to pray it along with the verses in Ephesians. Praying Scripture as a promise of God was still a new concept to me, but I clung to the promise that He would heal my brokenness and take away my darkness. As I prayed and reflected, I was overwhelmed by a sense of brokenness. I had never viewed myself as broken before and hardly knew where the feeling was coming from.

Looking back, I know that it was the feeling of one who has lived in a broken world. Like every other person who walks this planet, I had been exposed to the effects of sin: death, dying, pain in relationships, disappointment, and separation from fellowship with God. All these produced a broken heart because I had never taken this pain to the foot of the cross. I had never asked God to heal my broken heart. Instead, I buried the pain within, denying its existence. As a born-again Christian, I believed that I had a new heart in Christ and didn't have to ask for anything more; I merely had to accept waiting to get to heaven for wholeness in my heart. I didn't know how to believe that He would do this, but I felt this desperation rising within me. It was an intense need to be whole and to be released from my darkness.

One song that we sang in church was *Hear Us from Heaven*.[4] The chorus was particularly meaningful to me. It was a prayer asking God to hear our prayers and to touch our generation. I got down on my knees in church begging God, crying out in desperation. The sheer weight of darkness and confusion that I had felt in my life seemed to bear down upon me. It was the weight of a broken heart, crushed, just barely surviving, longing for wholeness. I wanted to

---

4   Anderson, J. (n.d.). Hear Us From Heaven. Retrieved June 2012, from Lyrics Mode: http://www.lyricsmode.com/lyrics/j/jared_anderson/hear_us_from_heaven.html

be free. I wanted faith that had substance. I wanted to know the promises of God in my heart, not just in my head.

Laying Out a Fleece

God did not directly answer my prayers in the service that day, but in my heart there was such a thirsting to know God. I had reached the end of my head knowledge; I knew that I did not know God in my heart. I knew that I was broken, desperately in need of the touch of the Healer. My Scripture memory, years of Christian reading, and devotion to Christian service seemed meaningless. These had brought me no peace or joy. I began begging God to show me clearly that He was active in my world here on earth. No longer could I be content with keeping Him boxed into the idea that only in heaven He works with power, that the only thing He does on earth is save a soul for eternal life.

The Lord heard my prayers and revealed to me in very clear ways that He was alive and well. He graciously gave me several real life experiences of showing Himself to me. In the Old Testament there was a warrior, Gideon, whom God called out to battle. Gideon was afraid and tested God with fleeces of sheep. One night Gideon left a fleece outside and asked that God allow dew to fall on the fleece but to allow the ground around it to remain dry. God did this. We all know that when dew comes at night, everything outdoors gets drenched by it, so clearly this was an act of God. The following night, Gideon put out another fleece and asked that God make the fleece dry and soak the ground around it with dew. God did this as well (Judges 6:36-40). Thus, Gideon's faith was strengthened. His heart trusted God, and he went on to do great work for God.

The Bible does not necessarily teach us that it is good to test God, but in this case God had compassion on Gideon because He knew Gideon did not have the faith to believe. I believe that, in my case,

God did the same. He knew I did not have any faith; I was crying out to Him to just show me so that I could have faith.

Over the course of a week or two, I began to see God at work in the circumstances of my life, little things like mysteriously taking care of a problem at work. My heart began to know that I have a Father who is good, who oversees all my life with tender, watchful, loving care. He was not a God seated far off in heaven. I would have noticed His hand at work in circumstances of my life long ago if my eyes and ears had been open to it, but I had been too busy trying to be a good Christian. I had always been too afraid that I might misinterpret the Bible or take something out of context, and so I kept the work of God confined to the work He did in the Bible. My belief had always been that when the Bible was finished being written, the active work of God on earth came to an end as well. He left us with the Bible as a guidebook of how to live righteously and to show the way to heaven. Now, for the first time, I began to understand in my heart that God is not confined to the Bible but merely defined by the Bible. The Bible shows His character, how He has worked in the past, and how He will continue to work in the future. As my eyes were open to the Lord at work on earth, my faith began to grow.

There was an altar call one Sunday morning for people to come forward who wanted to be healed of their broken hearts. I was really frightened to go up because the altar calls at this church were different from ones I was used to, but my desire for wholeness was greater than my fear. Over the course of my life, I had gone forward for a number of altar calls; always before, I had gone forward out of repentance or to renew commitment. Never before had I gone forward to receive from God.

I went forward, and I received. In a miraculous way I sensed a great light penetrating my heart. After all the months of praying for my heart to be flooded with light, it was! For the first time in my life, I felt a sense of faith that I had never had before. It was not faith that could be debated with intellectual disputes but faith that came from deep inside, from the unseen that had no basis for argument. I have little to say about how the faith got there except to say that I asked God for heart knowledge and He gave.

Loved

The love of God for humanity is woven throughout the whole Scripture, Old Testament and New. Many of these verses about God's love I had memorized and believed. However, there had not been any experiential knowledge of His love in my heart.

Envision for a moment a young married couple. If the husband verbalized his love for his wife repeatedly but never touched her, how do you think she would feel? Would she question his love? Would she wonder if there was something wrong with her? In order to hold the marriage together, the physical expression of love is needed. That's how God created us. How much more so in our Christian lives do our hearts need to be touched by the love of the Savior in order for all the verses about His love to take root?

For me, this was a time of knowing His love as a reality so that the character of Christ's love could become a reality in my heart.

Seeking God for Faith

For years I had attempted with human effort to make my faith real. I had been trying to believe in the Bible and to live in that belief. When I went forward that day, I laid aside all my years of head knowledge, not even knowing what I was asking God for, not knowing if it was proper theology to ask Him, but humbly I went, telling God I that didn't have the answers and that I was not capable of producing faith in my human strength. It was a setting aside of pride, setting the gaze of my heart on Christ alone and His ability to give me faith. For all of those years as a Christian, I had been studying the Bible and my flesh had been convincing me that

I knew God. Not only that, but I had lived as a Christian while not believing God for faith; I only believed God for eternal life. Paul wrote about the amount of faith God has given each of us, which very clearly states that God alone gives us our very faith (Romans 12:3). Never before had I sought God for faith.

I became like the woman in Luke 8:40–48 who had an issue of blood for twelve years. She presses through the crowd to touch the edge of Jesus' cloak. Power went out from Him, and He asked who touched Him. When she came to Him and admitted that it was she who had touched his garment, He told her that her faith had healed her. As this woman pressed through the crowd, I wonder how much courage it took for her to step out and touch Him. Perhaps she was afraid He might be unhappy with her request, or she may have been scared of what people thought of her. Unencumbered by her vulnerability, she set aside her pride and stepped out with faith. Maybe she had just enough faith in Jesus to know that He was a man of compassion and love.

Somehow, someway, that day I pressed through all my fear and my pride with just the tiniest bit of faith (which had slowly grown during the weeks preceding this altar call), believing that He could touch me. I had to press through my system of beliefs and ask myself if I believed that the God who gave me salvation for eternal life in heaven would also deliver me from the power of darkness here on earth. Did I believe that the power of the resurrected Christ no longer demonstrated itself on earth after the close of the canon of Scripture? Or was I willing to believe that here in twenty-first century America, God wanted to touch my broken heart? I clung to the little bit of faith that I had, believing that the heart of Christ was compassionate and loving, knowing that true to His character, He would meet me where I was at—the bottom—at the end of my faith. I did not really know the answers to my questions, but I was willing to set them aside and just believe. I had become nothing.

All my learning became nothing, and that is where He met me. There at the altar, I felt wrapped in the embrace of One who is Love, whose love has power over darkness, whose love gives faith. He gave faith to believe.

Not only was it faith that He gave me that day, but He also shined into my heart with His love and touched my brokenness. Through my many years as a Christian, my devotion to prayer and commitment to Christian service, my heart had never known the presence of His love. It was the brightness of His love that could take away my darkness and cure a broken heart. That day was a turning point for me. I wrote a short poem that afternoon.

> *Wanting to cry*
> *Tears of joy*
> *He's alive*
> *Yet hardly*
> *Knowing how*
> *The forgotten*
> *Emotions*
> *Those packed*
> *Inside me*
> *And so many*
> *Questions*

At the bottom of the page I wrote "The day of my turning point."

Joy

I felt joy in God for probably the first time in my life. I wrote a few letters to friends and told them how much joy I had found in God. I wonder now if they thought I was dramatizing my experience, but with the joy I had found rising up inside, I couldn't help but shout and sing to the world that I felt joy! It was a sensation unlike anything I had known before, true joy bubbling up out of my soul. The storm of my inner turmoil began to still and peace came, as joy welled up and filled the emptiness.

John Eldredge, in his book *Walking with God*[5], describes some of what I was experiencing as my soul began to be healed. He writes that often there are two sides to Christianity: one is the side of righteousness who are strong moral people, but often this is bound with guilt and shame. On the flip side there are those who preach grace, possibly to the extent that holiness is neglected. Mr. Eldredge is all for purity, except that we cannot get there until we have healing in our souls. I had lived long on the side of righteousness but only now was I embracing the healing that I could receive freely from God. I had always held myself up to a moral standard, but close behind this was guilt and shame. My attempts to live righteously always fell short of the standard, so I often felt that I had failed God. I wanted to live in holiness, but I had felt emptiness and darkness. Jesus' death on the cross was for my eternal life but also for victory over brokenness in this life. He died so I could be whole, set free, and filled with His love. No longer did I have to live bound by the chains of guilt and shame, insecurity and fear, which were the effects of sin; on the contrary, with Christ's victory over death, I was released from the power of bondage.

Questioning

This began a time of intense questioning, as my short poem had said "so many questions." God had been in this box I had created for Him. Everything I ever learned or memorized from the Bible had been to me doctrine, not the living Word of God. All the mighty acts of God in the Bible had just been stories to me because I had been viewing God through my natural mind. I realized that the Bible was alive and that there were promises that I could cling to and pray. Night after night I would lay awake, wrestling with my

---

5   Eldredge, J. (2008). *Walking with God*. Nashville: Thomas Nelson, 34–35.

faith and with the concepts that I believed about God. I grappled with every doctrine I had ever learned to find the living truth in it. Scriptures that I had known all my life began to take shape, and slowly I began to have a faith that was alive, given by God. For years I had struggled to pray because I had dead faith. All my knowledge was stemming from theological study, not from a heart that deeply knew and trusted the Almighty God.

As I began to know Him in my heart with the faith that He had given, the Bible became to me the sharp double-edge sword described in Hebrews 4:12. I now saw the Bible as a book filled with promises for victory in this life. My heart began to know the great power of God available for me today, now, and every day till I die. No longer did I have the empty feeling that I was living with no streams of living water running out of me. Faith was real, and faith was moving. The power of Christ's victory over death began to be a reality in my heart, not just in my mind. My heart embarked on a life of fellowship with the Son of the Living God. This fellowship is sweet enough to satisfy all my desires.

Light in My Soul

This was the first time I ever experienced light in my soul. Ephesians 1:18–20 took on new meaning to me as the eyes of my heart were opened. For years I had thought about God on a human level in my mind; therefore, I was not able to understand Him or His Word. I had read the verses of Scripture that say it is the Holy Spirit that teaches us, but I had never truly relied on the Holy Spirit to teach me anything. I had been a saved, born-again Christian, but I had lived enveloped in a cloud of darkness, partly because I had never understood faith outside the natural realm.

Danger of an Experience

We love mountain top experiences, enjoy the thrill of roller coasters, and are inclined to seek excitement. Revisit the example of a couple again, this time after fifty years of marriage. The years have tested their love. The wife no longer tingles with excitement at the husband's touch. If she told that to some people, she might be given the advice that the spark has died and she should move on to find fresh new love again. But she knows a deeper love now, one that has years of trust in her husband. She knows his character better now than she ever did. The excitement of young love has blossomed into a maturity.

Within the Christian life, the urge to live in the shadow of an experience, or to live continually pressing God for another experience, is part of our human nature. If marriage was based off the first tingling of excitement at our spouse's first touch, it would never grow into something much more beautiful. Even with my own fresh experience of Christ's love, it was tempting to focus on what happened or how it happened and to try to make it happen again. Immediately following this time, I went through a period of rapid growth but found myself falling back into the humdrum of the Christian life.

I began to ask more questions, wondering what the experience meant and if it was real. As I sorted through these issues, I knew that it was a real experience. It was like an embrace from God. He wanted my broken heart to be filled with a sense of His love. Through Scripture reading and prayer, I have come to believe that God wants all of our Christian life to be lived with a sense of His love, but not through recurring experiences. His Word repeatedly talks about becoming conformed to the image of Christ so that we might know Him.

The acts of being conformed to the image of Christ and of knowing Him are humanly impossible. But it is possible by depending on His grace to change us. Born in human flesh, we are so sinful, unstable, and arrogant that we think we can conform ourselves to His image. It is only an act of God that He transforms our lives to be vessels of His honor. The transformation process does not come through repeated experience but through the daily dying, the daily yielding control, rooting out all darkness until only He shines through.

My experience was a turning point, one that opened my heart to the reality of God's love and presence. As I felt the experience fade, I continued seeking to know Him. I wanted the reality of faith to burn in my heart and consume me. The Bible talks about the Christian life being filled with victory, joy, and peace, not just sometimes but all the time. As I pressed through the journey, I found deep hidden issues of the heart that keep many from knowing freedom in their Christian lives. Eventually, it comes to a point of decision. How much of ourselves are we willing to give up to know Him? Will we forsake all to follow? Do we truly understand how much the bondage of our flesh holds us back from a heart-filled relationship with the One we love? He wants to heal our broken hearts, demolish our strongholds, and set us free from our sinful nature, not so that we might live but so that He will live through us.

The journey can never be one of seeking our own glory, wanting to be free so that we might live to ourselves. If freedom and healing is real, it is for service to Him. We don't seek the embrace of His love for what He can do for us but because we love Him. We trust the character of Him who promised.

When my life became transformed by the power of Christ, I became a bond servant because I wanted to. I have seen the path of darkness (even as a saved soul) and know the way that leads to death. I have seen the path of light, which leads to abundant life.

Life Application Questions

1. Is the love of God a reality in your heart?
2. What beliefs do you have that keep you from seeking God for a touch of His love?

3. Read Romans 12:3. Do you believe that God gives us our very faith?

4. Read Hebrews 11:1. Ponder faith. Do you think faith is natural or supernatural?

5. Write a prayer or poem to God, seeking Him as the Giver of your faith, asking Him to heal any brokenness in your heart and anything else that you may be feeling after reading this chapter. Incorporate Ephesians 1:18–20 into your prayer.

CHAPTER 4

Understanding the Broken Relationship

I will give you a new heart and put a new spirit in you; I will remove from you your heart of stone and give you a heart of flesh.

~ Ezekiel 36:26

Now that I had awakened to God in my heart, now that I sensed there was more to my Christian life than I had previously experienced, now that I saw the light of God, the question of how I ended up in such darkness had to be answered. My search continued, leading me back to the beginning. I knew the story of the Fall well, but did I really comprehend its impact on my own sinful state? In order to better understand what occurred, I wrote the account in my own words.

A long time ago, at the brink of time, lived the first couple. Their world was beautiful, perfect. All of the best was at their fingertips. Sustenance was found in the amazing garden in which they lived – all was grown without the hard work of a farmer. Perhaps bears played with mice, and cats slept with dogs.

During the cool of the day, the man and woman walked in the garden with the Creator. He was the good Father watching over them. It was a relationship that knew no limits—had no secrets. Love flowed. The Creator spoke of the world and said it was good. They experienced a life of perfect fellowship with God.

There was only one rule in this paradise, one tree with fruit that could never be eaten without dire consequences. For a while the couple remained obedient to this rule, but one day the serpent tempted Eve. In murmurs the serpent spoke of the luscious fruit on this tree and told Eve that the Creator was only trying to keep the best from her, that she shouldn't be blindly obedient because she was missing out on some great food. Besides that, he convinced her of magical power she would receive from the fruit; when she ate it, she would become like the Creator, knowing good and evil.

Never before had the woman engaged her thoughts about this fruit. The rule had been not to eat, so she had simply obeyed. Now with the voice of the serpent ringing in her ears, she looked at the succulent produce with eyes of longing. In her mind she began to reason, "It does look good. In fact, it looks better than any of the other fruit. I bet the Creator is just trying to keep the best for Himself. My husband and I should be enjoying the best of our own garden. Besides, what could be better than knowing good and evil?"

Through reasoning, she convinced herself that the fruit was good. In one swift decision, she plucked two pieces from the overhanging branches. Quickly she bit into one and convinced her husband to eat as well. As they ate, the savor of the juicy food settled in their mouths. There didn't seem to be anything so bad about what they had eaten. They rationalized that perhaps the Creator had been mistaken about the tree. He could not possibly have meant for them not to eat of something so delicious.

Just as the last bites were in their mouths, they looked at each other and became aware of their nakedness. All this time without being self-conscious! This could not be right, they thought. Hastily they plucked leaves from a nearby fig tree, and the woman sewed a makeshift covering for herself and her husband. Before she could finish, they heard the familiar voice of the Creator calling from the other side of the garden. Almost instinctively, the couple concealed themselves behind a tree, for they knew they had disobeyed God. Their guilt was already imprinted on their hearts as they hid from punishment.

The relationship was broken—never to be the same. With the entrance of sin, a barrier was erected that brought darkness, distrust, and insecurity into the sweet fellowship they once knew.[6]

Two things stand out to me from this account. 1) The hearts of man became darkened to their own desires. 2) Fellowship with God was cut off by the entrance of sin. Until the reality of these truths sunk into my heart, I did not have a true picture of God's grace.

Darkened Hearts

The darkened heart that occurred when Adam and Eve ate the fruit had to do with their inner man. Separated from the glorious light of God, which is one and the same as His love, the human heart is self-centered, striving to protect itself in its own shame. Long ago the storm shutters closed on the windows of the heart and locked tight with the first bite of the forbidden fruit. Every heart for the rest of earth's existence will be born in fleshly nature. This

---

6   This story is taken from Genesis 2 & 3 with literary liberty.

barricade blocks all sunlight, stifling the inner life man in darkness. The natural course of man's thinking is twisted, thinking light is darkness and darkness is light.

Though I spent years reading the story of the Fall, it had an insufficient impact on my heart. I understood the consequences of sin that had separated me from God. However, my familiarity with the doctrine of sin deadened the reality of the desperate state of my own fallen nature.

My comprehension of sin had always been tied to what I did, whether good or bad. Did I lie? Did I steal? Did I keep the Ten Commandments? I never had trouble believing that I was a sinner. The books on prayer and holiness spoke to me of a level of Christian living that I had not yet attained. I was always asking God's forgiveness for not spending enough time in prayer, not dwelling on Him enough, and missing opportunities to witness. I was aware of sin in my relationships as well, continually feeling guilty if I had an argument with my brother or was sassy to my mom.

For a while I would daily pray Psalm 139:23 asking God to show me any wickedness in my heart, but I always attempted to do this work for Him. I would carefully look at my life and only see that I needed to try harder to be a better Christian.

The problem was I computed sin as actions. Never had I recognized that sinful flesh was the state of my heart. Even though I was saved, I was still controlled by the natural man I was born into. For me it was not the outward sins but the sins of the inner man that exercised my sinful nature. Every false motive, complaining attitude, and word of distrust was evil in the sight of God.

I had the vague sense that my inner darkness and turmoil was linked to sin, but this only drove me to strive further to fix the problem by my own efforts. Little did I comprehend that my heart was dark because I was born in the flesh! In my inner man I still operated out of my fleshly desires. All through childhood I had believed this truth, but I don't know whether it was the perception of sin from a child's mind that led me to assume I was not living according to the flesh or whether it was simply familiarity with this doctrine. Until each heart has a revelation of who God is and how wicked we are, perhaps the mind cannot understand the doctrine of sin.

Comparing my actions to the lives of others was yet another area that kept me in blindness to my own fleshly nature. When I looked around me there were always Christians who seemed more sinful than I. Therefore I reasoned, how could I be doing that badly? Once again, without a revelation of God's holiness on my heart, it was impossible to discern my own heart.

Broken Fellowship

When Adam and Eve lived in the garden, before the entrance of sin, they had an amazing relationship with God. To think that He walked with them in the cool of the day! They enjoyed His company, and He enjoyed theirs. It was a pure, sweet relationship. With the entrance of sin, this relationship was broken. When I accepted the sacrifice of Jesus' death on the cross, I stood in right relationship with God once again. But was I encountering the relationship He offered me?

As I lived out the Christian life, I sensed a small glimmer of light within that paled in comparison to the glorious light of God that I read about in Scripture. Yet, in the routine of Bible reading and church attendance, my fleshly nature began to deceive me into dullness, causing the powerful words of Scripture to lack the compelling force that would nearly catapult me forward into a relationship beyond my wildest imagination. Through no fault of God, I almost stopped seeking deeper fellowship and embraced the lie that I knew God as well as I could while on earth. As I read the stories of the Bible, the Holy Spirit quickened my heart to a fellowship more glorious and light-filled than what I was experiencing.

I had been taught that when the sinner repents, kneeling at the cross, repenting of a fruitless life lived for self alone, another name is written in heaven; the new life in Christ commences. At this point, the possibility of change begins. Why then did I observe only small amounts of change in my life and the lives of those around me? Like me, many whom I knew invested in prayer, Bible reading, Christian literature, and so much more. Was this not the way to cultivate the Christian life?

I knew I was saved. I attempted to grow in my Christian life, but I struggled with shameful secrets buried in the crevices of my heart and lonely longings that were not satisfied. With diligence I cultivated my Christian life, yet my heart felt empty. Taught that Jesus satisfies the deepest longing, I turned inward, thinking the reason for that aching emptiness was because something was wrong with me. Where was the Jesus who promised to fill me? This questioning led to self-condemnation and an inner life of judgment, further estranging my heart from the abundant love of God.

As knowledge of the Scripture and the character of God grew in my heart and mind, there still seemed to be a darkness that has not been overcome by the power of the cross. I questioned the verses of Scripture that yearned for something more, yet the subtle message of the religious culture around me whispered that I should resolve to wait for heaven to be free from the weights of my heart. There in the celestial city, my heart would be satisfied. This seemed too long to wait.

I believed that as a born-again soul, I had been transformed, and so I resolved to attempt to live the rest of my days disciplining myself according to the principles of the Bible, learning more verses, serving more . . . all the while stuffing my real self down inside, hoping to be able to lock it up in a hidden place where no one would find it. I took upon myself this cumbersome burden to diligently attempt to break my heart to become Christ-like.

That was the error in my thinking; it was backward. My heart was sinful, but valued beyond measure by the One who created it. The Christian disciplines were good, but the lie was that I could discipline myself—when only God is capable of bringing about the holiness I desired. When our hearts become consumed by the relationship with the Holy One, He burns out our fleshly nature by the brightness of His light, and we become more righteous in our actions because of the purification of the relationship, not because of self-discipline we have exercised.

The Heart of Stone Versus the New Heart

As I was pondering this chapter, the Lord brought to mind Ezekiel 36:26, which promises God will give us a new heart, put within us His Spirit, remove our heart of stone, and give us a heart of flesh.

The relationship with God that Adam and Eve experienced was one of perfect trust that had no inkling of good or evil. Once evil was known to the first couple, their hearts were turned to stone. Each became focused on self . . . trying to control circumstances, surroundings . . . hiding within. Self-preservation became the only way to live. The heart that was created to fellowship with God became focused inward, protecting its own and guarding itself from pain, and became an enemy of God.

This was the natural man, the man who could not fellowship with God because he thought he was equal to God. The natural man would try to reason his way through life based on what he could see with the natural eye, rather than believing that there is One who is able to work in ways not seen by the human eye but only seen by the Spirit of God.

The curse of this stony heart was passed on to all following generations. Each new life inherited this heart of stone, conceived with walls of shame and guilt already erected around the tiny soul. Yet, when we are saved, our heart of stone is exchanged for a new heart that becomes the habitation of the Holy Spirit. The new heart is a glorious gift, giving the hope of new life, new mindsets, and new patterns of interaction to all who receive.

The stony heart, which I had been accustomed to, was used to receiving information through the guidance and direction of my mind. My downfall was that I was trying to operate the new heart the same way. A.W. Tozer writes concerning the human mind "that it was not given as an organ by which to know God, and that it is highly unfit for such a task."[7]

Later on, Tozer also writes of how confidence in the ability of the mind leads to rationalism, in which a person attempts to know biblical truths through the mind alone. However, he cautions that some things can only be known as taught by the Spirit of God.[8] Knowing His Word enables me to know whether I am being guided by the Holy One or the evil one. Relying on my own understanding does not give me this ability.

The stony heart is guided by the human mind. My natural tendency was to rely on my mind. All of life, pain and joy, was experienced and rationalized through my human mind. Therefore, with ease I fell into learning the new life in Christ by means of the mind, attempting to purify my heart with the teaching of the Holy Book. The battle raged on inside me because my mind and heart warred against one another.

The Bible teaches that the head of the church is Christ (Colossians 1:18). Also, Scripture states the believer has received the mind of Christ (1 Corinthians 2:16). If the mind of man teaches the stony

---

7   Tozer, A.W. (1950). *God's Pursuit of Man.* Camp Hill, PA: Wing Spread Publishers, 76.
8   Tozer, A.W., 79, 80

heart, how much more should the mind of Christ govern the new heart? Who better to teach me of a relationship with the Living God than His Son? Who else could reveal to me my sinful state but the One who is holy? Must I not learn love from the One who is love?

In theory, I often spoke of Christ as my teacher, as my leader, but from experience I now know that it was my own mind. Learning to walk in ways unseen by my human eyes is like learning to walk again. Learning to know a love that surpasses human imagination is not always easy because experience tries to drag me back into hiding, afraid that the God of love and light might see my flaws. At times, trying to live the Christian life by human reason seems easier because I can be in control; we humans want to be in control. Only knowing Christ's love gives me the security to be vulnerable—I don't have to hide.

The Work of the Deceiver

Why did I fall into this major misconception? How was it that the truth of God's Word did not reach my heart? The one who spoke lies to Eve so long ago is the same one who speaks lies into my ears and yours.

1. Holding us in condemnation

Immediately after eating the forbidden fruit, Adam and Eve became self-conscious. Their guilt was already imprinted on their hearts. For the first time they saw they were vulnerable, laid bare before the holiness of God. They felt ashamed in the presence of the Almighty. Even after salvation, the enemy longs to hold us in the guilt of condemnation.

The instinct of the first couple to make a covering for themselves is an image of the way I attempted to hide the nakedness of my heart from God. Like others I struggled with pain, brokenness, fear, and insecurity, which left me with the feeling of open vulnerability. Though I no longer needed to live in shame because Christ paid the price, I still felt guilty. While held in guilt, I could not honestly look at the depravity of my sinful flesh; the weight of condemnation was too strong. This is where the enemy wanted me.

2.   *Clouding our thinking*

The enemy works over time to prevent the Word of God from coming alive in our hearts. From C.S. Lewis' renowned work *The Screwtape Letters*, I have a vivid image of the wiles of Satan. He is not threatened if we attend church and read Scripture so long as it does not take root in our lives. With a slight twist of truth, he convinced me that self-effort was the way to live my Christian life. For years he darkened my vision of fellowship with God. As long as the enemy could speak lies into my soul, confuse my thoughts, make me uncertain of God's voice, and stifle me with fear, I was held captive by the power of darkness rather than walking in the light.

On earth there will always be a careful balance that I must maintain in this area; never can I think that I am always operating out of the mind of Christ. As I grow, becoming more familiar with the mind of Christ; as I pray, abiding in the One through whom all power is given; day by day, I can live asking Him to open my eyes to truth. While I was unaware of my distorted thinking I did not comprehend my need to depend on Him.

3.   *Masking the nature of sin*

As long as sin was vague, as long as a sinless life was something I was attempting to attain, I had an incorrect view of sin. The evil one did not want me to understand the complete depravity of the flesh nor the ensuing separation from God. While sin was confined to my concept of it, I did not truly attribute my inner darkness as a result of sin. I could produce Christian actions but excuse my inner life as part of my personality, my past, or a number of other things. If he could convince me that my inner life of darkness had nothing to do with my Christian life, he could keep me from surrendering it.

The truth is that Christ came to deliver me from the power of darkness, to set the captives free (Isaiah 61:1). Darkness within has everything to do with our Christian lives, for light and darkness cannot fellowship together. Therefore, until I saw my darkness as the state of my sinful flesh, I did not seek to be delivered from it. Freedom from darkness is mine with the power of the resurrected Christ! It takes my unconditional surrender. I have to cling to Christ, feed my mind and my spirit the truth, yield control to Him, and He sets me free.

Rooting Out

This is not a complete list of the enemy's schemes. The point is that I needed to be aware and on my guard against him. This is a battle for my very life. In the following three chapters, I write in depth about several things that kept me from fellowship with God. I believe that these things had power over me because I did not know the truth about them. As I delved into my heart, searching for the roots of darkness, comparing my inner life with truth from Scripture, the Lord graciously showed me the attitudes and actions of a sin-filled heart that had to be surrendered to a holy God.

While I refused to root out my issues, they became like an infection spreading throughout my whole being, affecting all my other relationships. The process of rooting out was painful, time consuming, and also very deliberate. Opening my heart to Him came at a cost. That cost is dying—dying to the fleshly nature of the carnal man so that the heart can be filled with the glorious love of a perfect God. To die is to live.

Life Application

1. Reflect on the relationship Adam and Eve had with God.
2. How accurate is your concept of sin, based on Romans 1:20–23, 3:10–18, and Ephesians 2:1–10?
3. What you would like your fellowship with God to be like?
4. Let God quiet your heart. Ask Him to reveal to you your sinful nature, ask Him to help you be vulnerable, willing to root out any issues you may have.

CHAPTER 5

The Heart of a Modern-Day Pharisee

All of us have become like one who is unclean, and all our righteous acts are like filthy rags.

~ Isaiah 64:6a

When I observed the religions of others, the pious devotion with which my coworkers of other faiths practiced their beliefs, I noticed a great deal of resemblance between my practice of faith and theirs. The question lingered inside me, "If I have the real thing, if the faith I follow is true, if I have a living person inside of me, why is my faith so similar to theirs?"

Set of Rules

Unbeknownst to me, much of my Christianity was made up of rules . . . how much TV I should watch, how much time I must spend in prayer, how much of the Bible I must read in a day or in a year, how much I must serve in church, how many verses I need to memorize this month. Almost unconsciously, I adopted the norm of do's and don'ts in the Christian world. None of these things are necessarily bad; in fact, all of them are good things, but how they related to my relationship with God gave access for the enemy to gain a stronghold. Living with this religious structure as the focal point of my faith edified my flesh. The flesh loves control, even if it is in the arena of controlling the religious structure of one's life.

As I have sorted through my own heart, filled with self-righteousness and the bondage in which I found myself, I recognize three causes for falling into the pit of righteous deeds: an empty heart longing for God, a desire to achieve a successful Christian life, and a mask for guilt and shame.

The Heart Feels Empty

I was attempting to be righteous in my own strength in effort to please God and get closer to Him. Deep within the culture of Christianity, I believed the subtle message that if I would just do better and become more holy, I would have a closer relationship with God. I was always striving to live the consecrated, God-centered life because I felt I just wasn't good enough for a holy God.

Of course, there is some truth to that. As fallen creatures, we simply aren't good enough. But the very foundation of our faith says that because Jesus died on the cross for our sins, His blood covers us when we receive Him. I had been taught that when God looks at the saved person, He no longer sees our sin. Why then did I live like it was up to me to become righteous?

In my heart, I never truly embraced the truth that God viewed me as accepted. I am His daughter and am promised victory in this life. He has already said that He is well pleased with me. He never asked me to become righteous in my own strength but simply to follow Him.

The great problem was that once I was saved, there seemed to be this standard of ethics I had to live up to. To the unbeliever, grace is always preached: God doesn't care what you have done; He will forgive, just come to Jesus. But after salvation, there were these rules I adhered to as law. Done out of religious obligation, they fed my flesh, offering no grace but a means by which I could further gain acceptance (I believed) with God. These Christian duties are wonderful, godly principles, but now I realize that they must originate out of love for my Savior instead of duty.

All those years of my youth, I longed for God, hungry and thirsty for righteousness. Year after year I would make deeper resolves to follow God more, whether that meant more Christian books on holiness read, more verses memorized, or more time in prayer. Day after day as I sat in my prayer closet, I longed to feel God closer, yet I was living a religion filled with striving and self-effort. Where was the divine strength that I was promised? All my striving, though well-intentioned, resulted in an achievement-based religion.

Cultural Christianity

Growing up in the church, knowing the Bible, and doing "Christian" things was a culture of Christianity that was built around me. Faith became doing just because that is what had always been done, not because of a deep heart compulsion to do so. Now as a parent I am only beginning to recognize the sobering task before me of raising children who do not just do the Christian thing, do not just accept Christ as Savior and go on to live "good Christian lives," but who know that God is real. As long as Christianity was a cultural thing in my mind, the power of God was lost to me; I was only going through the motions instead of allowing the reality of the supernatural God to burn in my heart. Until my heart embraced God for who He is, seeing Him as He is, filled with a presence unknown to my human mind, I could only continue going through the motions.

Though Christianity is said to be not a religion but a relationship, because I treated it as a religion, it had only the ability to conform my life to a moral standard but no ability to transform my heart.

The Pit of Achievement

In grade school I was an excellent student. Every evening I would diligently complete all of my homework, turning in carefully written sheets to my teachers the following day. Almost always I would do the extra credit activities, not because I needed to pass the class, but just to make sure I was near the top. At the end of every semester, I took pride in my achievement. Scholastic success gave me a feeling of self-worth. This carried over into my spiritual life. I had a mental checklist of what I did as a Christian. Through this I built my own sense of Christian worth rather than looking to God in whom I already had value.

Also engrained in human nature is the desire to please, to win approval of men. Even within the realms of our faith, we are taught the verses saying not to seek the approval of men but of God. What if I was trying to seek the approval of God with man's ways? My focus was not on seeking the approval of the ungodly world, but I was trying to seek God's approval with the same methods I used for everything else in life.

Achievement in the world is through report cards, study, and hard work. These are good, but they are all done in human strength. Throughout the Bible, there is a strange twist on man's way of thinking. For some reason God always used those who were little or weak. He chose a boy to fight Goliath, and fishermen to be His disciples. What I failed to see was that while I thought I was able, I was useless to God. When I relied on my own ability to carry out spiritual tasks, I built confidence in myself rather than in Him.

Living Under the Law

I came to realize that I had read all those Christian self-help books and books on holiness for two reasons. The first reason was that I was hungry for God and did desire to be a good daughter. The second reason was the unconscious attitude that the more I read, the more ability I would have to become pleasing to God. Yet, the Word says that without faith we cannot please God (Hebrews 11:6). Would not faith be the ability to believe that it is only God who could carry out His good work in my sinful heart? Yet I was attempting to control my depraved heart through man's effort. Trying to become a good Christian had turned me into a person who lived under the law. Through all of my reading, I had never understood the principle that even though reading and studying is good, if done in the flesh it is worthless. Romans 2:23 asks whether those who brag about the law dishonor Him by breaking it. The pride in my heart over keeping the law turned me into one who was breaking the law.

I had read and studied without understanding that only the Holy Spirit can truly help us live a Christian life. Therefore much of this had been building up my confidence in my ability to keep the law. This acted as fertilized soil in which pride grew and flourished. I had put myself in control of my spiritual life, thereby breaking the law that I was trying to keep. As long as I believe that I am something, that I am capable of carrying out spiritual tasks, that I have become morally upright, that my life is being lived as a perfect Christian, I am fooling myself and not allowing God's grace to pour over my soul.

During the course of my many years of Bible reading, I had absorbed from my daily devotions only the parts of the Bible that had to do with keeping the law. I was not able to understand any Scripture that had to do with grace and always skimmed over those portions. Grace is a free gift. In the do-it-myself mentality, grace has no place.

In 1 Corinthians 2:26–31, Paul talks about how God uses the foolish things of the world to shame the wise so that no one can boast in his own efforts, completing the passage with the exhortation to boast only in the Lord. When striving in human effort, the work of the Holy Spirit does not fully take place. When we read and study the Word, it is only the Holy Spirit that can illuminate our hearts. All the study resources in the world—concordances, commentaries, Greek dictionaries—none of them can take the place of the Holy Spirit. Use of study books alone causes an excessive reliance on human strength, which would allow us to boast in our own strength.

The effects of all this was that I had created for myself a works-based salvation. Several passages of Scripture teach against this.

- Titus 3:5 says that He did not save us because of the righteous works that we have accomplished but only because of His mercy.
- Ephesians 2: 8–9 states we are only saved by grace which we have been given through faith, so that we will not be able to boast in our own works.

The living I had done for achievement was like keeping a score-card for myself as to how "holy" I was. It wasn't that I was doing it on purpose, but for some reason I felt the need to know that I was doing well being a "good Christian." I had been adding up my righteous acts as if I could earn the right to be a daughter of God, as if there was no need for grace. All the righteous things I had done had been feeding my flesh for years. A.W. Tozer writes of the curse that affects all men inwardly. It is the Christian ego that we must be aware of, better known in the Bible as "flesh." Tozer warns against this deadly enemy of our souls.[9] My study and diligence as a Christian had all been done in the flesh and had fed my Christian ego. It allowed me to feel as if I was a good Christian, perhaps a better Christian than others around me. I knew that I studied and sought God more than most people, so pride had grown in my heart. All this achievement and study, in fact my very Christian life, had actually fed my flesh.

---

9   Tozer, A.W. (2007). *God's Pursuit of Man*. Camp Hill, PA: Wing Spread Publishers, 26.

Good Works as a Cover-up

There is a popular Christian song entitled *Stained Glass Masquerade* sung by Casting Crowns. Well-written, it describes the masquerade that church can sometimes be. On Sunday mornings we get dressed for church, put on the suits and the dresses, and attend a service in the stained glass auditorium. We sit there listening to the message as if everything is okay, as if the week we have just lived has been perfect with no pain. For some reason we attempt to leave our pain at the church door for a couple of hours, then pick it up again on our way out, as if it is baggage to be picked up at our leisure. Instead of church being the hospital where healing begins, it becomes a stage where we live a fake good Christian life.

As I look back over my adolescence, I know that this was me. Week after week I sat in the church pew with questions that seemed to have no answers. At times the fear of eviction loomed over my head, and the continual lack of money plagued my life for years. I was broken. Hurting. My heart was crying. Yet, I stuffed all of it inside and played the part of the good Christian girl who learned the most memory verses, helped in church, attended every Sunday, never said a swear word, and always obeyed her mom. With this I attempted to blend in with the crowd of other Christians, hoping no one would notice. If someone did notice, what would I say? Vulnerability to my pain, exposing it to others, would cause further pain.

Over time I think that I got used to playing the actress on the Christian stage. It became so familiar that the feelings of being in pain were numbed. It was as if I could no longer feel it. When eventually the Lord, in His grace, brought me through a time of healing, I hardly knew why I was broken. Brokenness was a way of life, I couldn't feel anything. Not love, not peace, and not joy. Quite literally, I might have been a Christian zombie.

Isn't there a tendency among us to avoid exposing the ugly in church? We don't want to bring the tears in. But if our hearts grasped the real truth, that He died to heal the brokenness, would we act differently? There is sometimes an aura around church that dictates we must be proper, smiling, polite, and calm. This idea is based on the biblical descriptions of love, joy, peace, patience, kindness, and self-control (Galatians 5:22–23). In our failure to understand that only God can create this in us, through the work of the Holy Spirit, we endeavor to produce this fruit in our lives on our own. When we can't, the only resort is to fake it. After all, if we don't have these fruits, then we must not be good Christians. When we are broken, we simply cannot exemplify any of the fruits of the Spirit from the depths of our heart.

The End Result of Human Righteousness

Whether because we are seeking to know God through study or righteous living instead of seeking Him directly, whether we find ourselves living our Christian lives through human effort of scholastic achievement, or whether the good works we do are just a cover over our broken hearts, the end result is much the same: an increased, ungodly Christian ego.

As I was writing this chapter, I found myself wondering why the Pharisees acted the way they did. What prompted them to act pious and self-righteous? Jesus had such cutting words for them, calling them "whitewashed tombs" and "hypocrite" (Matthew 23:27). With ease I looked at the Pharisees with criticism, thinking, "They had no heart. Everything they did was to be seen by others, just the opposite of what Jesus taught. And they were the ones who plotted Jesus' death."

The Pharisees were the ones who intended to throw stones at the adulterous woman. They prayed on the street corners for all to see. When out in the marketplace, they prided themselves on their public appearance. How Jesus battled their thinking about the law! God's law of love was never in their hearts, only the letter of religion that called them to outward holy living. Years of practice had refined the art of good works, making these teachers of the law to sit on a pedestal above the average Jew of that day. All the while pride grew, the heart became darker and the ego more powerful, carrying the soul to a life of harsh religion.

Stepping back to examine my heart, I see how similar I became to them. Any form of self-righteousness results in pride. Even in the silence of my thoughts, I have compared myself to others and thought I was holier than they. When I do something good, the enemy tries to gain a foothold there. As cunning as a serpent, he whispers words of pride into my ear, much like the way he spoke to Eve when he told her that she should eat the fruit to be like God. I can throw out the words he speaks or I can dwell on them, taking pleasure in the fleshly feeling these words give, and open the door for Him to gain access to my heart.

Not only that, but in my desire to appear pleasing before God, other people became my mark of success. Looking around at the lives of other Christians, I compared myself in order to feel that I was doing better than some, giving me a sense of smug satisfaction at my "successful" Christian walk.

The Guarding of One's Heart

Steeped in Christianity since birth, I was not aware of the fleshly nature of a human heart. Church attendance was never a question; involvement was always required. I never rebelled but went willingly and listened attentively. The Word was absorbed, and in head knowledge I grew greatly. All the while I was careful to examine my actions to make sure there were no moral sins in my life. I attempted to live by the rules.

As I looked back, I had to ask myself why I was unable to see the roots of pride growing strong underneath the Christian façade. Born in the flesh, with the curse of sin imprinted on my very nature, I never gave God full access to shine the powerful light of His glory on my sin struck soul. God showed me the truth of Jeremiah 17:9-10; the heart is so desperately wicked, so deceitful. We subconsciously think that because of our salvation, our sin nature is dead. In reality we have all power over this sin nature, the power given by the death of Christ. But all those verses in the New Testament speaking of dying to self equates to this: a daily dying to the sin nature.

Rely on the Work of God

The belief that we have been in the church for "x" number of years and have prayed "x" amount everyday—which keeps us from struggling with the fallen nature of mankind—is false! Only the power of God in our lives keeps us from the struggle with sin. He wants the glory for our victory over sin, so He must be the One who makes us victorious. As humans we like to think in concrete ways, so we try to make a formula out of our life of holiness. The only formula that succeeds is to abide in Him and He will do the good work in us.

We might have the desire to hunger and thirst after righteousness (Matthew 5:6) and the desire to keep God's law. However, He wants us to desire Him even more than we desire those things. When we focus on God and stop trying to look for ways to produce the desired results, He begins to cultivate within us all the righteousness that we desire. According to God we already have all of His righteousness within us by the death of His Son (2 Corinthians 5:21).

When we become focused on producing righteousness in our own lives, we deny the power of the cross. Only when we come to the end of ourselves can we receive the gift that He gave. The very thought that we could produce a holy life through our own efforts proves that we are still living according to the fallen sin nature that relies on man's abilities. Through the humility of a heart crying out for help, a window to the heart is opened for God to work. We begin to get a revelation of our inability to carry out the laws of God, understanding that we are incapable of carrying them out in our own strength.

Man becomes moldable clay in the hands of the potter, and a righteous life is formed—a righteousness starting from the center—in the heart of man where the Spirit of God dwells. Through the yieldedness of the heart to the work of God, a miracle takes place. God transforms the fleshly heart to a heart that He leads in righteousness.

Hunger after God. Seek His face. He knows the hunger within for righteous living, and He promises that we will be filled (Matthew 5:6)—filled because He did the work, not because of ourselves. Until our hearts have a revelation of the Holy God, we struggle to comprehend how fallen we are. Through years of Christian living, a fog had been covering my eyes, preventing me from seeing how proud my heart was.

Life Application

1. How do you view your ability to live according to God's laws?
2. Do you see any areas of your life where you see your Christian ego at work?
3. Ask God to examine your motives for living the "good Christian life."
4. Spend time asking God to reveal to your heart who you are compared to who He is.

CHAPTER 6

The Christian Heart in Bondage

> It is for freedom that Christ has set us free. Stand firm, then, and do not let yourselves be burdened again by a yoke of slavery.
>
> ~ Galatians 5:1

Have you ever looked at your life and felt displeased with who you are? Do you withdraw from crowds, have a tendency to manipulate people around you, find yourself continually angry over the small things and preoccupied with what others think, or always feel that you aren't good enough? Are you beginning to recognize that you don't like the reactions you have? Are you listening to the soothing thoughts that tell you it isn't your fault, that you are only a product of your past and you just can't help it?

Do you ever feel controlled by raging emotions? Do you feel as if you have inner issues of fear, insecurity, guilt, shame, or anger? When bondage goes unchecked, it becomes accepted as a familiar friend; we do not recognize it but embrace it as part of our personality. We say, "That's just who I am."

Early in my journey of motherhood, I found this deep anger and frustration escalating within. I had everything I had ever dreamed of: a husband, a home of our own, and an infant son. Life was good. But something was amiss in my heart. The cloud of darkness from earlier years seemed to be returning. I found my inner thoughts raging over the smallest things. Rising from deep buried places, voices spoke to me about my lack of worth. I was dissatisfied with my role as a wife and mother, thinking that I was called for more than this.

Were they all lies? Where did these raging emotions come from? They rose with no forethought, and I felt little ability to stamp them out. I knew that unless I found answers, I would only pass my own issues on to my children.

As I struggled against the darkness, God was faithful and provided a way of escape. Even now there are times when rampant inner emotions sweep me away and cause me to react out of feelings of fear, guilt, and shame, but God has caused great victory in this area of my life. I have experienced freedom, but I often find myself digging my heels in to fight as I stare bondage in the face. While on earth, I do believe I will always have to be on guard against the enemy of my heart. The good news is the victory has been won on the cross. I know my Savior has triumphed, that He is stronger and I have nothing to fear, so I can fight with courage, knowing that His will is for me to be free!

What Issues Did I Have?

Some of my issues were fear, insecurity, guilt, shame, and anger, which are all acts of my flesh (Galatians 5:19–21). All of them stood to testify against the knowledge of God in my mind. Fear lacks faith. Insecurity is concerned about self and what others think. Guilt and shame (going hand in hand) do not truly embrace the blood that washes away my sin, and tries to make self acceptable with human effort. Anger is often self-focused and comes when it does not get what it wants.

As a child I reacted normally to the pain and adverse circumstances in my life. My fleshly reaction was automatically to protect myself. Therefore through the course of my childhood and adolescence, these issues gained a stronghold in my heart. As an adult, I recognize that I must seek God, asking His help to break down these strongholds.

Often people don't believe they can change, so they don't even try. The battle is lost. Many think if victory over these issues is not visible at salvation, then it is not for this side of heaven. Instead of fighting for freedom, there is acceptance of bondage. Until I recognized my responsibility to break down the strongholds that kept my heart in bondage, I could not move forward in Christ. He held out victory to me, promising that He has defeated the enemy. I needed to grab His hand, walk beside Him to freedom, and cooperate with Him in this battle as well.

For this, the battlefield is my mind.

Understanding My Thought Processes

Throughout the years one favorite passage of Scripture that I memorized was Romans 12:1–2. Renew your mind. I thought that only included keeping myself from lust, not coveting, and not thinking evil of someone else. What about engaging my mind in excessive concern about tomorrow? Commonly called worry, Scripture directly commands against it (Philippians 4:6–7). What about the random negative thoughts that would pop into my head? What about entertaining complaints about life and my circumstances? I had a vague sense that these were not godly and would try to stifle these thoughts, but I never experienced any victory until I read *Who Switched Off My Brain*, by Dr. Caroline Leaf. While I was only trying to suppress negative thoughts, I could not deal with the root of the issues, so it was more like stuffing a jack-in-the-box back in the box, knowing that it would only be a matter of time before the box would be bumped in such a way that the lid would pop off and the jack-in-the-box would leap from within.

In her book, Dr. Leaf writes about the complex memory system of the human mind and the manner in which we absorb and translate our life experiences into our memory. If we are reacting to our negative emotions, then we build negative thought patterns, living in a state of reacting to the pain of our memories. In summary, Dr. Leaf writes that we can bury our emotions, but when we do so, the emotions we have buried remain alive. Therefore, our mind perceives this stifled emotion as fear. Consciously, we can deny the painful emotions, but after doing this for a time, it will become an automatic reaction.[10] When it becomes an automatic reaction, we live reacting to what has been buried alive within our hearts. The suppressed, negative feelings have become like a faulty operating system of a computer, always running in the background almost unnoticed, yet feeding our souls a self-destructing virus that will at worst cause us to crash and at best will keep us from victory in any area of our lives.

The good news is that with the power of Christ, I began to reprogram—or as Scripture calls it, "renew" my mind—so that I did not live the rest of my days automatically reacting to my painful memories. With Christ I could heal, I could take captive my negative feelings and emotions, bringing them to the foot of the cross and asking Him to take them from me. For a very practical, scientific explanation of how the mind works with these issues, I highly recommend Dr. Leaf's book.

As I began the process of working through the buried issues in my mind, I began to closely examine my thoughts, attitudes, and

---

10   Leaf, D. C. (2008). *Who Switched Off My Brain?* Dallas, TX: Switched on Your Brain USA Inc., 78.

words. When I found myself feeling fearful, I would ask God to show me the root of it, and He would show me numerous fearful memories that I had buried alive. If I found myself discontent or angry, often that too I could trace back to a distant memory in my past. It was hard, soul-wrenching work to think through the pain that had been squelched within for so long. Some thought patterns, memories, and actions I could sketch through my family line. Understanding my own thinking helped me to recognize issues of previous generations. Looking backward helped me to look forward, revealing to me that if I did not break free from bondage, it would be passed on to future generations. With determination I prayed that God would show me the path to freedom.

What I realized was that every thought within me that was not in line with what God said about me was sin. Every concerned thought about the future that was not according to the promises of God from Scripture had to be cast down, because my negative, false thoughts were more real to my mind than the truth of God's Word. Unconsciously, I made decisions based on my feelings of fear, guilt, insecurity, and shame. I had thought I could do nothing about this except try to live a good Christian life. Until I decided to rely on the Spirit of God to help me with the biblical practice of renewing my mind, I would not be able to write this book today.

Fear

Fear is in the middle of the night when the downstairs floor creaks, jolting us awake; when the figure in the checking account is less than the bills; when a loved one's health seems to be on the decline; when the political culture of our country seems bent on evil; or when the news reports of school shootings, child rape, and cold-blooded murder. Fear is the emotion grabbing our hearts like a wrench, tightening around the vessel flowing with our life blood.

Fear closes our hearts off from the peace and strength offered us through our relationship in Christ.

I knew this feeling well. Something in life would trigger feelings of fear, and I could feel the constricting anxiety rise within. I needed to recognize these thought patterns. When circumstances brought frustration, change of plans, or bad news, did I speak words of faith or fear? My spoken words were clues to what was in my heart, for out of the heart's overflow the mouth speaks (Luke 6:45).

What situations trigger fear in my heart? Lack of money has been a big one for me for a long time. Growing up with little, at times wondering where food was coming from, living through many moves and even eviction, the slightest hint of financial insecurity rocks my boat. When I first joined the working world, I worked to be the best, to please the boss, to be the most docile employee. Why? Because deep inside, fear dictated that I must. The uncontrolled voice of fear told me that if I didn't do this, then I might lose my job and once again be in danger of losing income necessary for my survival. Looking back, I realize that many decisions of life came from my unacknowledged need to feel financially secure.

Through the past few years, I have learned to interact with my fear when it comes to grab hold of my heart. The Bible tells us that the enemy is on the prowl, looking for someone to devour (1 Peter 5:8). Fear was an area he had succeeded in devouring me, literally eating up true fruit in my spiritual life. While I lived in fear, I could not move forward with the Lord. In Scripture, the illustration is used that blessing and cursing cannot flow out of the same mouth, for salt water and fresh water cannot flow from the same source (James 3:8–11); similarly, I wonder how fear and faith can flow from the same heart.

Guilt

There are two areas of guilt that are prevalent within Christian circles.

1. Guilt as it relates to service

    How often do we do something out of guilt? I always had this motivation. For a long time, I was unable to say no to the needs of others. I took on the responsibility of their happiness. Whether in work, church, or at home, I was usually the one to immediately comply with the request of another, to the extent that I had few boundaries. God never gave me the responsibility of ensuring another's happiness.

    It was with this sense of over-responsibility that I served God. As if I was entrusted with His pleasure. For years I felt guilty that I was not doing enough to serve Him, not living sacrificially enough. Guilt dictated my service to Him, not love. Every time I heard of a mission trip or service opportunity, I would think that maybe He wanted me to serve in this area. Often I would begin the process of signing up for the task but then would begin to feel inundated with all the responsibilities in my life. The thought of adding another task overwhelmed me, and I would withdraw from this opportunity. This further added to my sense of failure and worthlessness to God.

    My tendency to overcommit comes from a desire to please God. I continually have to remind myself that God does not intend for me to run myself ragged, neglecting my physical body, or ignoring the needs of my own spirits, for quiet before Him.

2. Guilt as it relates to the desire for holiness

    I desired to live the Christ-life, a life of holy living. I confused self-righteousness with the righteousness that only God has given me to live out. Through the teaching of Scripture, I learned the rules of our faith: do not lie, do not commit adultery, do not swear, do not watch shows that are bad for your mind, do not entertain coarse joking, but do read your Bible, pray, go to church, and repent continually. These rules had attached themselves to my heart and dictated my actions.

Guilt came as a quiet voice, disguised as conscience, and I lived according to the law rather than the love of Christ. The balance of law versus love had gone off-kilter and rested on the side of the law alone in an effort to gain holiness through personal striving. This type of guilt expanded deep into my inner life, leaving me with a continual feeling of unworthiness and self-loathing. Often it was projected into relationships around me.

Recognizing Guilt

Guilt produced compulsive actions as I compliantly followed its tormenting voice. It took work to come free from guilt, but through the power of Christ, I did and continue to do so. The battle is never over but must be fought until the end.

As I continually committed myself to God to work through the process of sorting out healthy actions and doing away with unhealthy ones, I saw tangible victories. These were signs of God's faithfulness that I clung to. The first step was to acknowledge that though my outer actions looked Christian, the root of them was not based on truth but rather on condemnation.

As Christians we need to know who we are in Christ. We are set free, liberated, covered with the blood of the Lamb, and called sons or daughters. There is no condemnation after salvation, and we are set free from the law of death (Romans 8:1–2). Guilt often came because I did not recognize it as the voice of the enemy but assumed that it was the voice of the Holy Spirit correcting me for sin. Wanting to become Christ-like, my desire was to become obedient to the Father. Yet without discernment, I compulsively obeyed the lies of the evil one.

Anger and Insecurity

Two other areas of Christian bondage are anger and insecurity. Beth Moore writes an amazing book entitled *So Long Insecurity*. Through reading it, I was able to gain greater insight into the workings of the human heart. I lived many years reacting to how I felt about myself, worrying about what others thought, and sub-consciously acting in ways to validate my existence. I believe that the only cure for insecurity, like the rest of these things that hold a heart in bondage, is a revelation to the heart of who God is—of His amazing love for me!

As I examined the words coming out of my mouth, the Lord showed me that they were often harsh, snippy, and critical, and they came from a root of anger. I believe my anger was a by-product of fear, guilt, and insecurity, stemming from the discomfort these issues were causing my heart. They gave me the feeling of being bound-up, unable to go forward, locked in a cage. As I was incapable of verbalizing these feelings, the only outward sign was anger. Repeatedly the anger went unchecked because I did not know the source of my anger and was too broken to be vulnerable to others trying to help me with it.

Anger is not always sin. It is part of healthy emotions. When I feel anger rising, I need to find the root of it and deal with it in the appropriate way. Anger that was continually stifled formed a raging undercurrent in my heart. It was not meant to be an incessant expression of my everyday life.

Three Observations on Bondage

Only the Spirit of God can make the Word alive in my heart; only this can change my life! Just knowing the words of Scripture was not enough to heal my brokenness. I struggled with this because in my heart I did not truly have a revelation of who God is. So broken, hiding within, I had closed my heart off from God Himself. I was afraid of vulnerability. I have learned that I must continually pray that He, the Giver of every good and perfect gift, will make the Word alive in my heart, asking Him to show me the path to freedom.

I have three observations on the bondage I experienced.

1. *Bondage went unrecognized.* As long as I was attending church, studying the Word, and not living in outward sin, I assumed that I was doing well spiritually. I had lived with bondage for so long that it became a way of life, not recognized as something to commit to Christ.

2. *Bondage was rationalized and condoned.* Even though I had the vague sense all was not right in my walk with the Lord, I had the underlying belief that, because of a person's past circumstances or family upbringing, this is "just the way things are." Until I grasped the truth that Christ died for my heart to be free from the strongholds of the enemy, I could not have victory in this area. I had to embrace the truth that His blood shed on the cross was enough to liberate my captive heart. He never intended for me to wait till heaven to break free from this bondage.

3. *Bondage was not treated as a sin.* Bondage is opposite of truth, opposite of the freedom Christ died to give me. Therefore, if I deliberately continued to live in bondage, unwilling to work through issues, it would have been a decision to remain in darkness, captive to the enemy's schemes. If lying, stealing, and viewing pornography are associated with the dark works of the evil one and a lifestyle not acceptable in Christianity, why would the dark works of the same enemy that occur hidden in the heart not be equally unacceptable?

The Effect of Bondage of the Spiritual Life

Bondage was not treated seriously earlier in my life because its effects on my spiritual life were not clearly seen. While these issues had a strong hold, my thought life was overcrowded with negative emotions. The thoughts and negative emotions served as voices inside my mind, giving direction to my course of action. No matter how sincerely I may have wanted to walk in God's will, His still quiet voice could not be heard over the clamor created within my mind by these issues. Anything that gives direction to my life besides God's Spirit and His Word must be put to death. I could not coddle my issues and expect to grow spiritually.

As I look back at my frustration with knowing God's will, I believe the bondage I was in kept me from clearly discerning the will of God. Envision for a moment that there is a conduit between the mind and the heart. When my mind is clear, free from issues, there is a flow of communication between the Spirit of God dwelling in my heart, and my human mind. The Spirit does not dwell in my mind, but when the conduit is open, my mind becomes His. He is able to direct my steps, quietly speak to me about the issues of bondage, and I enjoy open communication with Him. When the conduit is open, my spiritual life is enlarged through such a relationship. While I was living in bondage, allowing thoughts and emotions contrary to the Word of God to go unchecked, the passage of communication between the Holy Spirit and the mind was blocked. Willfully or unconsciously, I chose to listen to the lies, allowing them to become truth to my heart, grieving the Spirit of God.

Even though I desired with all my heart to follow God, I did not recognize the work of the evil one in my thought life. My assumption was that since I was diligently engaging in the Christian disciplines of prayer and Bible study, my relationship with the Lord was what it should be. I did not comprehend the evils of the human heart, the strong bent toward the flesh. The prophet Jeremiah speaks of the deceitfulness of the heart (Jeremiah 17:9); only when the holy light of God shines on the darkness of my heart can I begin to understand how deceitful it is! Even though I may have unwittingly allowed bondage to form in my life, bondage has been the natural course of humanity since the Fall. As a redeemed child, I have His supernatural power over the otherwise natural path of destruction.

All these issues stem from the heart of flesh. Fear at its root believes that man is in control of life rather than God. Guilt and shame do not truly accept, from the heart, the sacrifice of Christ on the cross. Instead, the responsibility to become holy or acceptable to God rests in human hands. Insecurity looks inward rather than upward for approval. For each one the emphasis is then on human control, which ultimately is the result of the Fall of man; when the fruit was eaten, man would become like God, knowing good and evil. Since then, humanity elevates itself to a god, trying to take control of life.

The Effect of Bondage on Relationships

There are two great commandments in the New Testament. The first is to love God and the second is to love our neighbor. In the paragraphs above, I hope you can see my inability to love God and have open communication with Him while in bondage. The other point I make is that I could not fulfill the second commandment of loving my neighbor while in bondage either.

The only one who can truly teach me love is the One who created it: God, the Maker of heaven and earth. While the conduit of communication between self and God was blocked because of my issues, I was unable to learn love. This is how bondage affected my relationships with others.

- *Barrier between people*: In my own pain, I tried to keep others out; therefore, in all relationships I attempted to protect myself, rather than looking out for the good of others.
- *Put up a façade*: I was unable to interact as the person God created me to be because I was insecure and didn't want others to see the real me for fear I might not be accepted. Only in Christ could I truly know who I am. Therefore, I could not be real because I did not know my own identity.
- *Withdraw from fellowship*: I kept people at a distance. My relationships were mainly shallow. I was ashamed of my own issues and did not want others to get close enough to notice.

Responsibility to Break Down Strongholds

Regardless of what our strongholds are, Jesus said that if we want to be His disciples, we must take up our cross daily and follow Him (Luke 9:23). With deliberate actions we must engage in battle with our thought life and ask the Spirit of God to show us hidden issues of our past that might be holding us captive. This is a daily responsibility. It might involve pain to work through issues that have been buried for years, but it is God's will and God's command! The hardest part is at the beginning of the journey when we recognize how many issues we have condoned, accepted, and embraced for so many years. It may take a long time because this is a spiritual battle. The enemy does not want us to have victory.

Renewing our minds requires engaging with your thoughts and asking the Holy Spirit to reveal truth. We are told to think on those things that are noble and pure (Philippians 4:8). Fear, guilt, insecurity, and anger are not noble and pure. These things are going to come into our minds as normal human emotions or reactions, but our responsibility is to refuse to allow them to have place in our lives.

As the Holy Spirit revealed my issues to me, I never felt condemned but only in need of repentance. I felt forgiven and set free.

Life Application

1. Are there any areas of bondage that might have been revealed to you through reading this chapter?
2. What is your concept of the Romans 12:1–2 principle of renewing your mind?
3. Are the contents of your thoughts noble, pure, and true?
4. Ask God to help you work through your past and to give you strength to renew your mind and discernment to recognize what is not godly in your thought life. Praise Him for the power He has made available to us to overcome.

CHAPTER 7

The Confusion of Distrust

Abram believed the Lord, and he credited it to him as righteousness.

~ Genesis 15:6

As I was taking up the fight against fear, the most powerful weapon I had was Scripture. Yet as I tried to quote Scripture to myself, I was shocked to recognize that I hardly believed the verses I was quoting. All those years of listening to the issues of my heart had taught me to distrust God Himself, as though a cloud of confusion interfered with our relationship. Just as a house divided against itself cannot stand, a heart divided cannot stand either. I could not serve a God I did not trust. Like a vicious cycle, when I focused on my circumstances, fear took hold, and I gave way to distrust in God.

But how was I to learn to trust God?

Reacting Based on My Perspective

The first several years of married life went smoothly; I was in control and had little to trust God with. But, when the figures in the checkbook became a little bit smaller and the bills a little bit higher as our family grew, and I knew God was calling me to give up a steady paycheck to work from home to be with my young children, doubts grew in my mind. How was I to trust when I couldn't see the way? Past experience held me back, fearful the outcome of God's leading would be unpleasant. Did I believe that God is no longer for me and that His character cannot be relied on? In earthly wisdom I had often attempted to rationalize why God allowed certain things to happen, as if knowing the answer would calm my heart.

Reacting or attempting to justify life in view of how I saw things was a vain attempt, especially when my heart still lived in a state of perpetual bondage and there was so much baggage blocking my relationship with God. While in bondage, as much as I tried, my heart could not enjoy sweet communication with Him. The darkness of bondage has little fellowship with the Light.

Unaware of the effects of sin caused by the Fall, my heart unconsciously absorbed information about the Almighty through the perception of human experience. Perhaps it began with my father's death while I was still a child or came to fruition when my lofty dreams of youth died, causing my heart to question the goodness of God. Though I continued in church-attendance, Bible reading, prayer, and the Christian disciplines, unperceived by all was a heart that no longer had unwavering trust in a God who is good. I had allowed doubt to grow from buried questions never put into words.

The Age-Old Question: Why Bad Things Happen

My father, a good Christian man, died at age thirty-six, when I was seven years old. My heart began to form conclusions about God, life, and death. Though saved and in the process of learning the Christian faith, my heart felt gripped by this pain. I wanted to question why God would let a good man die. Why would He leave two young children and a widow without a man of the house? Yet, ashamed of my questions, I buried the doubts and pushed forward toward a future of Christian servanthood.

Job is the most frequent example in the Bible of a man who suffered greatly but did not turn away from God. I notice how Job cries out to God, voicing a litany of questions, doubts, anguish, and pain. In the end, God answers Job and challenges his faith. Job even admits that he was questioning things too far beyond his own understanding (Job 42:1–6).

Eventually I arrived at this same place of questioning. Job pressed through to God, desperate for answers, pushing through his anguish to touch the Living God who knows all things. Job didn't receive answers to his questions; he never was told why all that happened to him, but his heart received a revelation of who God is. This was enough to turn his heart from doubting to faith.

Merely reading the story of Job could not dispel the anguish of my heart, but following the example of Job did. My relationship with God was not real until I came to Him with everything, asking, pressing, wrestling with faith. He did not reveal to me why circumstances occurred, but in the same way that God spoke to Job's troubled heart, He spoke to mine. Job records that his ears had heard of God, but only now had he seen Him (Job 42:5). Is this not what Paul prays for the believers in Ephesians 1?

Through wrestling with faith, my heart received a revelation of the holiness of God. My questions were answered by the very character of God Himself. Knowing Him, knowing the character He has revealed and the love He pours out on me, became enough to answer my questions because my heart had a fresh knowledge of the holy. His name that is I AM, Jehovah Jireh, Jehovah Rapha—these names are the promise that He provides, He heals. This was enough for my heart to encounter the character of God that will not change. When the names of God became imprinted on my heart not by my own ability but by His still quiet voice, my questions fell silent.

My Personal Dilemmas with Trusting God's Will

Another question that I had concerning God's leading came as a result of a mission trip when I was sixteen. For several years I had wanted to go on a mission trip with a certain teen mission organization. Finally, my mom agreed to let me go. I could barely contain my excitement! Since childhood I had been fascinated by missions and third world countries. I had read countless missionary stories, and when I heard of a mission trip to Papua New Guinea (PNG), my interest was perked. Having read Don Richardson's missionary books about tribal New Guinea, I felt this was the place to start going to the ends of the earth for God.

I signed up for this summer trip about six months prior to departure. All school year I prepared, doing a huge school project on PNG. I also dedicated extensive time each morning before school in prayer for my team and the trip.

This mission organization had scheduled a two-week boot camp to equip the team members for the field. While at boot camp my excitement mounted, as did my dedication to doing whatever God wanted me to do with my life. A day or two before my team was supposed to leave for PNG, we received word that our visas did not come through. I thought this was just a stumbling block that Satan was using to deter our mission. After meeting together as a team for prayer, our leaders decided that we would fly to Australia, which was en route to PNG, and wait there for our visas to arrive.

When we arrived in Australia, we settled at the mission's headquarters while the leaders worked to get our visas. Word arrived that the visas would be issued, and we began preparation to travel to PNG. However, the embassy closed that day without issuing the visas, so it was decided that rather than wasting more time attempting to get the visas, we would stay in Australia and serve there for the remainder of our time.

I didn't get it. I did not feel led to Australia; I did not want to be there. I had agreed to go to a third world country for God, not Australia. Besides, I had prayed so much about this trip; didn't God answer prayer? Did I just not understand His will for me? What was I supposed to believe about God from this? This caused great uncertainty for me as I grew older. I felt unsure how to pray or that perhaps I just didn't understand God. I felt I didn't know what to pray for.

Unbeknownst to me, these questions about God's character that lay unasked at the bottom of my heart were corroding my relationship with Him. Stuffed into a dark corner of my heart, I attempted to bury them, ignore them, pretend they didn't exist, and just go on with the Christian life. It didn't work. They just sat in the recesses of my heart, eating away at me, questions that poisoned my heart while unanswered. This clouded my perception of God, pulling a veil over my eyes, blocking His light from coming in. My spiritual eyes became faulty, like bad eyes that cause the whole body to be filled with darkness (Matthew 6:22b–23). I viewed God through a soul filled with unanswered questions and doubts. A faulty view of God had flooded my soul with darkness.

The Basis of God's Work in Our Lives

All too often I have looked to Romans 8:28 as the guidelines for how life should be as a Christian. Since God works good, my assumption would be that life would be good. The natural man in me always wanted to believe this meant God would work my circumstances for good—my definition of good. But what if the truth is that I don't know what is good for me? The Bible also says that discipline is not pleasant when it takes place, but God disciplines us for our good so that we can share in His holiness (Hebrews 12:10b). If I think about being a parent and disciplining my children, I know I don't always let them have what they think is best for them. Often I don't give them what they want because I know it is not good for them. If they don't learn self-control at a young age, they will never become responsible adults. So what if that is true with God? How does that apply to my faith?

What Is God's Will?

Slowly I began to understand the purposes of God. He is all for His glory. And as a Christian, the thing I desire most is that God be glorified in my life. This is why we are taught to pray that His will be done on earth as it is in heaven (Matthew 6:10). I had not been seeing things through an eternal perspective but only through eyes that thought I knew what was comfortable here on earth. But what exactly is His will on earth as it is in heaven?

In the book of Romans, just following the promise that God works for the good of those who love Him, comes a verse that says that He has predestined us to be conformed to the image of His Son. This is the will of God for me; that I would be conformed and transformed to the image of His Son!

Bad things had happened to me in my life, and I didn't un-derstand the goodness of God because I viewed Him through my pain. The Bible was clear about God being good and about Him working things for good according to His purpose. The choice was mine. Either I was going to choose to believe God, or I was going to choose to continue to view Him through my life experience.

As I dwelt I began to see that it is through my choice to trust Him that God can begin to work for good. As soon as I am will-ing to see that He is going to work it for my good and His glory, He can begin that work that He wants to do in me, whether it is through the refining fire of unpleasant circumstances or whether it is through comfortable ones. I have an entire book, called the Bible, filled with the promises of God. I had to make the choice to believe the promises of God even if I didn't see them. Is not faith being sure of what we hope for and certain of what we do not see? (Hebrews 1:1) When I believe that the end result is Christlike-ness, I become sure of what I hope for. Then I can humble myself before God, asking Him to teach me through the situation. As I do this, I also know that I am praying God's will be done rather than simply praying that the circumstances change.

Often I had been so caught up in the mindset of why is this happening to me and what can God do with my life that I had failed to understand that God is working for kingdom purposes and eternal value. He holds the world in His hands, intertwining the life and circumstances of each person for kingdom purposes that I cannot see from this earthly perspective.

I can choose to believe that God worked my father's death for my good, so that I might be refined, that I might draw closer to God. I can choose to believe that God did not want me to go to Papua New Guinea that summer when I was sixteen because He had lessons for me to learn while in Australia. As I look back, I believe that God taught me many lessons in Australia. The first lesson He taught me was that I don't need to go to the ends of the earth to serve Him. The third world mission field had been somewhat of an idol to me and a means of earning God's favor. God had to strip this mentality out of me so that He could create in me a pure heart with pure motives. Every time a hard thing happens, whether it is as simple as a tough day raising children or being stuck in a roadblock, I have the choice to allow God to use it for good in my transformation process.

Distrusting God

If I allowed myself to continue to live my life with a faulty view of God, I would always remain ineffective. That is because I truly did not trust God. In my mind I had been trying to get close to Him through all the books that I had read and the Bible I had memorized, but I could not draw near to Him because my heart had reservations about His character. I felt as though He had failed me, and this distrust grew, causing a chasm in our relationship. Just as with a friend who has betrayed you, you withhold from this person the deep issues of your heart. In a sense this was how my relationship with God had been. I could not be vulnerable because I did not trust Him.

This distrust of God is an age-old tool of deception used by the enemy. In the garden Eve heard from the serpent that if she ate the fruit, she would know good from evil and be like God. She chose not to believe that God's command was for her own protection. Distrust began that moment. Since the Fall, our old nature continually leads us to believe that we know what is good for us. I had a hard time believing Romans 8:28, that God works all things for my good, because in my mind it wasn't good. My mind looked at the natural rather than looking at the supernatural, spiritual transformation that God was and is working in my life.

My belief in all the truths of Scripture was subtly eroded because of this distrust. I unconsciously viewed every promise of the Bible through eyes that were uncertain about God. My self-worth that God has revealed in Psalm 139:14 was drowned by distrust, for if I did not trust God in His entirety, how could I believe what Scripture teaches me about myself? This was just another area where the stronghold of insecurity controlled me.

My view of the purposes of God was all messed up. I was always trying to make God work in my circumstances and basing my trust of Him on that. My questions about His goodness had to do with what I could see from an earthly perspective but not what God could do to refine my heart from His perspective.

As I've grown and worked through the issues of my heart, this would be my commentary on Romans 8:28. When a hard situation comes into my life, I want to grumble and complain, "Why did God let this happen? How can this be for good?" While I continue to grumble and complain, I remain defeated, and God doesn't seem to do anything with my situation or with my relationship with Him. As soon as I tell Him, "Lord, I know you are in control. I believe you can work this situation for my good and that you can teach me your ways through this situation," then He begins to work. However He doesn't necessarily change the circumstances that are causing me pain; rather, He begins working on my heart, showing me bad attitudes, false motives, lack of trust, and better ways of extending grace to others. Before He changes anything in my circumstances, He begins the refining process in my heart.

Over the past several years, I have noticed that God doesn't always use bad circumstances like sickness, financial hardship, or outward affliction to refine me. When I begin to fight the battle within that afflicts me daily, I am constantly growing, drawn to the foot of the cross for daily sustenance because I know I am not able to fight the enemy of my heart on my own. Awareness of the inner battle calls for a relationship dependent on the work of God for every moment of life. When I have myself in proper perspective, as a creature born in the flesh, fighting for the life of my spirit, I know that only God can deliver, change, and transform.

To have a good relationship with God, I have to choose to believe that He is good and that He is working for my transformation so that I might become a person conformed to the image of His Son, which will bring glory to His name. Believing that He knows what He is doing when I can't see it. This is what I love about Abraham: he believed God. All he had was a promise, yet he believed that God was leading him out of his country, and he believed that he would become the father of many nations. The act of believing was credited as righteousness (Genesis 15:6). Like Abraham, I have God's promise, one that says I am predestined to be conformed to the image of His Son. The choice is mine to believe.

Also, I can choose to believe that through any trial He can bring me closer to Himself. The Bible talks about the refiner's fire, so that we might come out like gold. Even the psalmist wrote that it was good to be afflicted in order to learn God's decrees (Psalm 119:71). Therefore I can choose to believe that God is trying to teach me something. I can choose to submit to God's work in my heart, praying that He will teach me His way that I might walk in His truth, asking for an undivided heart (Psalm 86:11).

My desire is to draw closer to God, learn more of His ways, and become more Christ-like. With Christ, death to the flesh equals life to the spirit. He will do whatever it takes to cultivate my heart to know Him. As a Christian I live with an eternal soul, which will live in heaven forever after my days on earth are finished; therefore, God's plan is to better equip me to serve Him in eternity. He works in me to purify my heart in order that I might come forth as gold.

Warning Against Unbelief

The New Testament contains a strong warning against unbelief. The writer of Hebrews reminds us of the rebellion of the Israelites in the wilderness, how they hardened their hearts in unbelief. In anger, God declared that they would not enter into His rest (Hebrews 3:7–12). It was so easy for me to read this passage and think that it did not apply to me because I had been a Christian all my life. I had gone to church faithfully and had always prayed. But it did apply to me. Questioning God in my circumstances while I was being tested was just as the Israelites did in the wilderness. Over the forty years that they were in the desert, God continually showed them His mighty power, but they so quickly forgot and hardened their hearts. It was hard to trust in the Promised Land that they could not see. All they had was the promise of God. While they wandered in the wilderness day after day, they had to learn to depend on God for daily food. A year or two or ten of trying circumstances seems so hard, yet if I look back over my life, I see can see His faithfulness even when I did not trust Him.

Day after day I have choices to make: will I believe God or my circumstances? When I choose to focus on my circumstances, I view life as a trial, and my heart quickly turns to unbelief, thinking that God is not working. I am coming to realize the flightiness of my human heart, which is demanding of the now and restless with any waiting. It balks at the affliction because the outcome of becoming as gold seems so hard.

As I choose to dwell on God's goodness, faith rises and reminds me over and over how God delivered me out of bondage and set me free from my flesh. Is not this the faith that can move mountains? The unbelief that I struggled with earlier in my life has no place because confidence in God's love and goodness has taken its place. I can choose to trust one step at a time as I believe in the work of God. There are still many days that I struggle to believe, wanting to complain, yet I remind myself of the faithfulness of God. This too is a discipline, a choice.

Life Application Questions

1. How do you perceive the working of God in your life's circumstances?

2. Do you struggle to trust God? Are there questions that you have about His trustworthiness?

3. Read Romans 8:28–29 and summarize it as it applies to your life.

4. Pray and ask God to give you the proper perspective of Him and His work as well as the proper perspective of yourself. Confess any areas of pride or distrust.

CHAPTER 8

The Restored Relationship

And I pray that you, being rooted and established in love, may have power, together with all the saints, to grasp how wide and long and high and deep is the love of Christ and to know this love that surpasses knowledge – that you may be filled to the measure of all the fullness of God.

~ Ephesians 3:17b–19

With proper perspective of the full impact of the broken relationship between God and man that occurred in the Garden, I looked at the restored relationship with fresh insight. Before sin entered, Adam and Eve fellowshipped closely with God. In vague terms I understood that their connection with the Father seemed much closer than mine, but why? They knew the love of God and enjoyed deep fellowship with Him. These were missing links in my own walk with God.

What Is the Love of God?

There is a great deal of difference between knowing about God's love and experiencing His love firsthand. As I read Ephesians 3:17–19,

I knew that I had no concept of His love for me. I felt nothing long, wide, deep, or high concerning His love. In fact, I didn't feel it at all. These verses became a prayer. I asked that I would know the love of God that surpasses knowledge.

My first encounter with His love was at the altar call I described in chapter 3. Since then He has shown me His love many times in numerous ways. Most often it is through the orchestration of time or circumstances in such a way that I see His hand at work and stand in awe that He cares so much about my life. Or in the quietness of my workshop, He draws me to remembrance of Him, filling my heart to overflowing with His love. One morning during my devotional time, I had such a strong sense of His love that I wrote the following poem entitled *The Love of God.*

The river of His love
Sweeps me away
Caught in a current
Of purest delight
Carried by power
Unknown to my mind

His love pours in
Radiance explodes
Embracing His love
My heart beats to His
Unable to contain
The touch of His love

His love pours over
And rising within
Is Christ in me
The hope of glory
Swelling my heart
Bursting with joy

This is the love of God that fills me and captivates my heart!

His Love Relates to Our Adoption

I have heard that it can take time for adopted children to embrace the love they receive from their adoptive families. Perhaps because of their past abuse, these children cannot comprehend the unconditional love extended to them by their new parents. For this reason, they may hold themselves apart from their new family until trust is gained. ✗

The imprint of my fleshly nature was still on my heart. Therefore, the reality of what He did for me, that He paid a price I could not pay, that I did not have to strive to please Him, did not dawn upon me. I always feared His wrath, believing if I made one wrong move, He would severely punish me, or if I did not walk in His will, He would never give me a second chance. My eyes and ears were not open to His love because of my fear of the vulnerability of being loved and ignorance that I was not living in His love. I lived as an adopted child who had not opened her heart to the One who adopted me.

The Power of His Love

I was always restless, anxious. I wrestled with the meaning of life, with my purpose here. I felt lost in the world, without an identity. Now, as He pours His love into my heart, I find my identity in Him. I am His beloved. When I know this from the depths of my heart, I know who I am.

I am a desperate creature who is so needy for love. When someone speaks a cutting remark, instantly my reaction is to feel unloved. I can choose to let this feelings fester in my heart, or I can turn to God. Before I knew my own brokenness, I simply could not comprehend the power of His love. I was unaware that I longed for love.

Over the years, Walt has talked to me a great deal about a person's ego structure. Basically, it amounts to a person's value of themselves—their sense of self-worth. At first I did not understand my own need to feel worthwhile. Deep within is the desire to be accepted. Only in God's perfect love is this need satisfied: the need to be loved unconditionally, fully, passionately. Only God's love can truly fill my heart with the value I longed for.

Even to this day, with my life filled with marriage, children, and friendships, I notice that I can rely on these relationships to meet all my emotional needs for love. However, if I do, it saps the life out of them. My expectations are too high. No human relationship can fill my heart with the love that I need to thrive.

When my heart lives in this place of safety, love from others does not affect my self-worth or sense of well-being. In His love I can freely love others because I am not afraid of man's opinion or in need of man's affirmation. Many books address the subject of how to better love in relationships and how to overcome feelings of being unloved from childhood, but this sets the expectations of love on an earthly plain. No matter how much I cultivate my personal relationships to love, it is only the love of God poured into my heart that will truly meet all of my emotional needs.

His love is not a passing emotion of the day but is a consuming presence, resounding assurance, every moment of each day if I will but dwell in His embrace. Strength, direction, and resolve to overcome my past, present, and future are a result of having His love as the focal point of life. His love is a sure foundation. Apart from this, I only know the power of my flesh that drives me to be self-focused, pulling me off course from God's plan for me.

The Love of My Father

Even as a parent, much focus is given to making certain that my children feel loved. Though it is a tremendous responsibility to raise children, I realize that I am not capable of making certain that they feel loved. I can ask the Lord to help me love them to the best of my ability, but also I can teach them that only the love of God will satisfy their hearts completely.

Recently I have been listening to the audio version of *The Five Love Languages of Children* by Gary Chapman and Ross Campbell. Throughout the first chapters, they discuss a child's need to *feel* loved, not just to *be* loved by their parents. Every child is created differently and has a main love language that speaks love to them more than the others. When children feel loved, they are more emotionally stable and respond better to discipline.

Though I strongly believe in parental responsibility to love children to the best of the parent's ability, ultimately a child cannot rely solely on a parent's love to assure all his or her emotional needs. I can ask the Lord to help me in loving my children, but I can also teach them to seek God, who created their hearts, with their specific needs. I will fail them. Only their Heavenly Father can meet every need of their hearts.

It was not until my early twenties that I felt loved by God. I knew all the verses about His love, but they had little meaning to me. God is the perfect Father, and He designed our hearts with the need to feel His love just like a child needs to feel the love of their parents. He knows the emotional needs each of us has. Regardless of our past or present, He is able to supernaturally satisfy our hearts with His love.

Just like the child that could not respond well to discipline because of feeling unloved, I could not face my sinful heart for the same reason. Without the love of the Father poured into my heart, I could not bring my sinful flesh to Him for transformation because I feared His wrath. When I know His love, I come to Him as a repentant child, knowing that He will forgive me and continue to love me.

Why Didn't I Feel His Love?

Since God is the perfect Father, one might ask why I did not feel His love even though I was His child. James 4:3 stands out in my mind; it says that we do not have when we do not ask. I never asked God to shine His love in my heart. Paul prayed over the Ephesians that they would know the love of God. These were born-again Christians like me who did not know His love. In the same way, I needed to ask God to show me His love or else I could not know what He was waiting to pour out in my heart.

Even now there are days when the love of God does not seem as real to me as others. Once again, I find myself at the foot of the cross, praying that He will show me His love, that He will fill my heart with the knowledge of His love. If I do not ask, I do not receive.

The Perfect Love

As you likely know, 1 Corinthians 13 is the most frequently quoted chapter on love. I always held this as a standard to live by—that I must discipline myself to love so perfectly. I always failed. I could be patient sometimes, but not always. I enjoyed getting my own way. Sometimes I rejoiced to see bad befall someone who had not been nice to me. I couldn't do it; I couldn't carry out this standard of perfection.

For some reason, I had interpreted this chapter more like the Ten Commandments than as a love letter from God to me. To think that God loves me with patience, that He never gives up on me, that His love never fails. I do believe that God intends for me to live according to this chapter, but it is only when His love fills me, when I know my sheer inability to carry out the task of loving that I come to Him in desperate need of help. Then by the power of His Spirit, He does a mighty work in my heart, and through me He lives His love out to the world.

The Purpose of God's Love

A header above Ephesians 3:14–20 in the New Living Translation reads, "Paul's Prayer for Spiritual Growth."[11] The passage that follows is his prayer that the church of Ephesus would know God's love. Never before had I thought of knowing His love as a means for spiritual growth. As I reflected on where I have come from, I realized that until I knew the love of God from my heart, I remained stagnant in my spiritual growth.

The following are a few Scriptures that speak to me about the purposes of God's love.

- John 3:16 – He loved us to save us from eternal separation from Him.
- Jeremiah 31:6 – His love is the means by which He draws us to Himself.
- 1 John 4:7 – He loved us so that we might love one another.
- 1 John 4:18 – His love casts out fear.

I needed to know what these verses meant in my life, so I compiled the following list.

- They teach me who I am in Christ, sealing my identity in Him. His love fills my heart with the knowledge of my adoption. I AM HIS CHILD. That is the only identity I need in this world. I belong to my Father.
- They give me the courage and power to face my issues (fear, guilt, insecurity, shame, anger, etc.). His love is the force behind my journey.
- They fill my heart with the capacity to love others, which carries out the second commandment to love my neighbor. In my interactions, I see how much my human ability is lacking. I cling to Christ and ask that He would fill me with His love so that it might pour out to the lives around me.

---

11   *KJV/NLTPeople's Parallel Edition.* Tyndale House Publishers. Carol Stream, IL. ©2005.

- They fill my emotional needs so that I am not solely reliant on earthly relationships for love. This keeps me from becoming a needy person, looking to those around me for a love they cannot give.
- They provide a foundation on which to build fellowship with God. His love is the link to knowing Him. Because I know His love, I long to be with Him.

Fellowship

This last point is crucial to my relationship with God. There are two aspects to my desire to fellowship with God: I desire fellowship while on earth, and I long to be with Him in heaven.

The Desire for Fellowship

Since childhood, I have spent time each morning in prayer and Bible reading soon after I wake. I believed through this that I would enjoy fellowship with God. But often my morning devotions seemed like a one-way communication of me trying to get to God. In my quest for His presence I wrote:

Deep unquenchable longing
For quiet before God
Searching for His presence
A yearning to see His face
Only in the stillness
Can I hear His sweet voice
Only in silent moments
Does He whisper to me

The poem continues, but this portion reflects the longing for a deeper relationship with God, to know Him. As I have learned His love, the longing is filled but also draws me back to Him continually.

There are days and weeks when I feel drained. My heart is restless, anxious, burdened with worldly cares. I know that I am not resting in the presence of God. Like the psalmist I come to God, longing for my thirst to be quenched (Psalm 63). At these times I love to go to a large hill nearby. It overlooks the valley in which I live. In this place, looking down at life, with the beauty of creation surrounding me, I sense Him closer than ever.

Though I love to take time apart from my schedule to climb this hill, I am learning that fellowship is even more than that; it is the continual need of my heart to listen, to abide, and to dwell in His love. When I rise in the morning to write, when my plans for the day get changed by an emergency, when I interact with my family—every moment is an opportunity to commune with Him. As soon as I stop focusing on Him, my heart becomes anxious over the little things in life. Fellowship is broken. He cannot fellowship with me when my thoughts are not resting in His peace.

Time after time, I lose my focus. The practical application of Philippians 4:6–8 must take place. I can't train myself to refrain from anxiety or to be thankful in all things. I cannot cultivate the peace of God that I long for. But I can recognize my sin, ask forgiveness, and entreat Him to help me maintain a steady gaze on Him. He does the work, and I do the asking. As He faithfully grants my request, forgiving me for my failure, fellowship is restored once again, and my heart rests in His peace.

Lack of His peace is a sure sign that I am not fellowshipping with Him.

The desire for fellowship has become so strong that it is more like desperation. The vitality of my life depends on it. The new man that we are in Christ cannot live without fellowship.

Fellowship as It Relates to Anticipation of Heaven

As I understand the life that flows from fellowship, my heart longs for heaven. It is no longer merely linked to wanting to have earthly cares done away with, but now I long to be with the God I love.

Wanting to be with Him forever reminds me of my engagement. I remember how Tony and I wanted to spend every waking moment in each other's company. We counted down the days until the wedding ceremony, anticipating when we would be joined together forever. It was our love for one another that gave us the anticipation. I felt loved by my fiancé, I heard him speak of his love for me, and I knew I was his choice for a wife.

If I did not have unwavering confidence in Tony's love for me, if I was not acquainted with his character, I would not have desired to spend the rest of my life with him. Until the love of God was deeply rooted in my heart I had the vague sense that I should look forward to heaven, but there was no anticipation of being with Him. I knew a lot about Him, but until I began to enjoy true fellowship, I did not know Him in a personal way. When I know a person, like them, and have confidence in their character, I seek to spend time with them. Such is the case with my relationship with God.

Knowledge of the depths of God has awakened in my heart. How far beyond my imagination is the King I worship! During my earthly life, before I see Him face to face, I relate to Him through the eyes of faith and through the Spirit He placed inside me. As my heart dwells in His presence, I have found fullness of joy, but I feel tugged by the weights of this world. Oh to think of heaven, when I will be in His presence forever! I know it will be more wonderful than I have ever dreamed.

The Restored Relationship

I have found the relationship with God that I longed for. The sacrificial death of Christ provided a way for me to know His love and to fellowship with Him all of my days. Like Adam and Eve, I too can talk with Him continually, uninhibited. It is no longer a one-way relationship. He speaks to me as much as I speak to Him. Not in audible words to be heard by my physical ears, not always in vocabulary that I can put into words. Through illumination of the Scripture, affirmation of His love, and a constant awareness of His presence, I hear Him with the ears of His Spirit within. He alone gives the ears to hear.

Life Application Questions

1. Do you have a sense of God's love for you?
2. Do you long for deeper fellowship with God?
3. What is your anticipation for heaven like?
4. Pray that God would open your heart to His love and to greater fellowship.

CHAPTER 9

Depending on the Holy Spirit

But the Counselor, the Holy Spirit, whom the Father will
send in my name, will teach you all things and will remind
you of everything I said to you.

~ John 14:26

Above all other religions the biblical teaching of the Holy Spirit is
unique, but the promise that He will guide, comfort, counsel, and
teach us was a nebulous doctrine rather than a living reality in my
life. There was a mystery surrounding Him that I did not understand. I could talk about the essential truths concerning the Holy
Spirit, but they were not truths evident in my own spiritual life. I
never felt dependent on Him, as if He was a vital part of each day.

The Holy Spirit Is a Person

Part of knowing the Spirit was acknowledging Him as a person—the living person of the Godhead dwelling within me. I looked
at the doctrine of the Spirit through abstract lenses rather than
viewing my relationship with Him as a personal interaction. Our

relationship with Him is personal because He has the following characteristics of a person:

- *He has a voice.* His voice speaks to my spirit. He always speaks in line with the character of God and through Scripture. It is my responsibility to be listening for His voice and to pray diligently that I will hear when He speaks.

  In John 10, Jesus spoke of the sheep recognizing the voice of the Shepherd. While in bondage, I did not hear Him because I was entertaining the voice of the stranger.

  I struggled with guilt for a number of years because I confused the voice of the Holy Spirit with my own overactive conscience. False guilt could make me believe that I was obedient and humble, but guilt always condemns. However, when the Holy Spirit is the one convicting my heart, there is immediate restoration at the time of repentance. The Holy Spirit never condemns me for not being righteous, unlike guilt. Instead, He imprints on my heart the truth that God has already pronounced us righteous by the blood of Christ, and when fellowship with Him is broken due to my sin, I can repent, immediately experiencing reconciliation.

  Learning to recognize the voice of the Spirit is a process of Christian growth. James 1:5 promises that if we lack wisdom, we should ask of God. Even now when I am uncertain of His voice, unsure that I am hearing correctly, or wondering if I am hearing Him at all, I ask God for wisdom.

- *He has a presence.* The Holy Spirit has a presence that can be felt just as real as the presence of a person. When I am alone in a room and someone else walks in, even if I didn't see the individual come in, I feel the presence of a person. In the same way, the Holy Spirit has a presence in my heart. For a long time it was only a theological concept to me, not something that I had experienced in my own life.

My relationship with the Holy Spirit is much different than I ever imagined. During pregnancy, I felt the movement of my unborn children. The activity in the womb testified to me that the baby was alive and healthy. Similarly, the Holy Spirit dwells and moves in me. As I begin to recognize the presence of the Spirit, His movements become familiar. Sensing His presence within becomes the norm rather than the exception. I notice discernible signs of life as He actively stirs my heart. If I do not sense Him moving, I look to God, asking Him to examine my heart for issues of sin that may be quenching the Spirit.

The movement of the Spirit within and the awareness of His presence are the companionship God promised me. His presence is the deposit guaranteeing my eternal life in heaven (Ephesians 1:13–14) which gives me the assurance that He will never leave me (Hebrews 13:5). God understands that my heart is lonely, in desperate need to be filled. Therefore, He gave the Holy Spirit to be my constant companion.

Once again, this relates to the bondage of the heart. My heart has the capacity to hold only so much. I cannot be filled with bondage and be filled with the presence of the Holy Spirit. He is repulsed by what is not holy. Bondage is of the enemy, but the Holy Spirit will not use His power to free me from bondage unless I ask.

In 1 Corinthians, Paul speaks of the body as the temple of the Holy Spirit, exhorting believers to act in ways honoring to Him (1 Corinthians 6:19–20). While Jesus was on earth, He also confronted sin in the actual temple, angry with those perverting it with dishonesty, cheating, and selfish gain (Matthew 21:12–17). Both these examples show me how important God's dwelling place is to Him. My heart is a dwelling place of the Holy Spirit. God desires it to be a place fit for His presence. If I allow the bondage a place in my heart and do not ask Him to rid me of it, He does not have a pure temple in which to reside. God does not expect me to have a perfect home for His Spirit, but He does expect me to work with Him on the housecleaning.

The Work of the Holy Spirit

Each person of the godhead has unique responsibilities. Three tasks of the Holy Spirit are teacher, intercessor, and guide.

Teacher

The Holy Spirit teaches me many things if I will listen for His instruction. The following are several areas of His teaching:

- *Scripture*: One of the greatest experiences of my journey has been the Holy Spirit teaching me the Bible. I have always loved Scripture, but I never knew it as a book that was alive. I studied it as a textbook for holiness. It was words on a page, like any other book I might read.

  The Holy Spirit ignites the written word of God, transforming it into the living Word of God. This living Word is the food my soul longed for. The written Word without the teaching of the Spirit did not assuage my hunger, but with the Spirit it becomes food that satisfies, giving my soul the nutrients needed to become spiritually mature. God never intended for me to rely on the words of Scripture as the reality of His promises but to stir in my heart a desire to see the promises alive in my heart, brought to life within me by the breath of the Holy Spirit. Now as I read the Bible, He brings living application to my own life. When I ponder the lives of the Old Testament patriarchs, He brings them to life!

- *The Love of God*: In Romans 5:5, Paul writes that the Holy Spirit teaches us of God's love. This is yet another area to depend on Him. Without the Spirit, I would never have known the love of God my Father!

- *Spiritual things:* Previously, I had leaned on scholastic study to learn the faith. Yet, the mystery of Christianity is that only through the Holy Spirit can I learn of spiritual things. As I read 1 Corinthians 2:12–16, I more clearly understand that God does not expect my natural man to comprehend the spiritual things; therefore, He gave the Holy Spirit so that I might depend on Him to teach me what I cannot learn by my own efforts.

Intercessor

To think that prayer is not entirely my responsibility is freeing. How often I have felt compelled to pray for someone or for a situation only to find that I did not even know how to pray. The Bible promises that when we don't know what to pray, the Spirit makes intercession for us (Romans 8:26–27). Previously, I assumed that this was an automatic occurrence, that He knew when I didn't know what to pray and that somehow it was happening without my awareness of it. As I meditated on these verses, I began to ask Him what to pray and to admit to Him that I don't know what to pray for. There are so many situations in life for which I don't know the purposes of God.

For instance, there is someone dear to my heart who has cut off communication for a long period of time. Daily this person is on my heart. I long to make continual intercession for this one, but I don't even know what is going on in this person's life right now. I do have Scriptures that God has given me to pray but more than that, I find myself continually telling Him that I don't know how to pray. As I do this, I literally feel Him making intercession for this person in a powerful way that I could not put into words. This is the power of the Spirit's intercession. He is all-knowing; therefore, He knows this person's situation, hurts, and needs. With His omnipotence, He intercedes much better than I, but He uses me to ask Him to pray. I am not the one doing the work. He is. My work is to ask Him.

I used to make a vast list of prayer requests including people and situations. I relied on the lists to make sure I was a good prayer warrior. Rather than depend on lists, I am learning to seek His help in intercession. Then He frequently impresses on my spirit specific things to pray for, or He directs me to pray verses of Scripture that I would not naturally have turned to.

Guiding My Heart

He is the faithful guide of my heart. Drawing from the soothing words of the psalmist, He leads me, like a sheep, beside quiet water, and in green pasture (Psalm 23). If I follow His guidance, He will keep my heart in a place of quietness, free from the clamoring anxiety and activity my mind is capable of. In order for Him to lead my heart, I have to relinquish control of life.

The more I know God, the more I am aware of the flaws of my natural mind. It completely opposes the peace that is in God. Many of my thoughts are focused on excessive concern with the next moment and how to fix a problem, myself, or someone else. My mind focuses on the activities of earth's existence rather than on the purposes of God's kingdom, thereby putting my priorities in the wrong order. As He guides me, showing me moment by moment the priorities of eternal value, I have to willfully cooperate with Him, turning my attention away from my worldly concerns. This does not mean being slack about work or life's responsibilities but involves continually entrusting those things to His care with confidence that He will order my steps in these areas as well.

Without the divine guidance of the Spirit, I cannot be free from the pressure of this life that robs me of the peace He longs to bring to my soul. The more peace that I experience in Him, the more aware I am of the destructive nature of anxiety. Anxiety hinders fellowship with the Spirit and hampers spiritual growth.

Guiding the Activities of Life

I wanted clear direction for the activities of life. The Bible promised that the Holy Spirit would lead me (John 16:13), but I had felt no supernatural sense of direction, which frustrated me. I have come to know the guidance of the Spirit in a much deeper way. He is involved in every moment of my life when I let Him. There are many instances in which I know His direct guidance. These are several examples.

Just before my husband and I started dating, the Spirit laid it on each of our hearts to make a Christmas card for the other on the same evening. We were only acquaintances at the time and had no logical reason to exchange Christmas cards. I was the deli cook, and my husband was a customer. The next day, we handed each other our cards at the same time. This was the beginning of our courtship. I don't like to wonder what would have happened if both of us had not listened to the prompting of the Spirit.

In the middle of writing this book, I felt the need to have someone help with the reading and the flow. I didn't know who to ask, but He put two older, respected women on my heart. It never would have occurred to me to ask either of them. It turned out that one of the ladies had helped with the editing of her daughter's book and was already well-prepared for this task. Without the direction of the Spirit, I would never have taken this step and would have been robbed of the spiritual input these two women gave.

Many times I have known His guidance in work. There have been several decisions that humanly I never would have had the courage to make. Like taking the leap into self-employment, but the Spirit impressed on my heart a confidence in His leading. Also,

He prompts my heart in daily interactions with clients as He opens the door to conversation, bringing glory to Himself.

A clear example of the Holy Spirit orchestrating events is in Acts 8:29–30 when He directs Philip to come near the chariot. This is a testimony that He is able and willing to direct the encounters of my life. Several times I have needed to go to the grocery store for a last minute dinner essential, grumbling as I went. The Spirit prompted me to turn to Him, asking Him to use this time. While in the store or in the parking lot, I have encountered someone who I have been praying for but had not seen for a long period of time. I believe that He directed me to be in that place at that time to be a blessing to those individuals.

His guidance frequently comes as a strong impression on my heart. It is very different from the prompting of guilt, which brings the feeling of torment. There are times I hear Him prompting me to do things I feel uncomfortable doing, such as sending a card to someone I hardly know, putting my hand on a friend's shoulder while I pray for her, or starting a blog when I know nothing about social media. In all these cases, my flesh tried to weigh me down with the worry of "What will people think of me?" Most often it is the desire for men's approval that attempts to pull me from following the Spirit.

Cultivating a Life of the Spirit

Cultivating a life attentive to the Spirit is now an essential part of my Christian life. These are several things I have learned to attune my heart to His leading.

1. Become a student

- *A student studies:* I had to study His voice, observe the manner in which He operates, so as not to confuse the work of the enemy with the work of the Spirit. This is altogether different from reading the Bible but involves prayer and a heart bent toward God.

- *A student is teachable*: From the example of Psalm 25:4, I look to God and ask Him to teach me through His Spirit. I cannot come to Him dependent on spiritual knowledge that I have but must come to Him in spiritual poverty, knowing that I do not know the answers, that in and of myself I know nothing. All spiritual learning comes from Him.
- *A student recognizes the Teacher:* John 14:26 tells us that the Holy Spirit will teach us all things. I enjoy listening to sermon podcasts of various speakers while I work. However, I constantly have to guard my thoughts from leading me to believe that I need these to grow spiritually. Listening to Bible teachers is good but cannot take the place of the Holy Spirit. In fact, only the Holy Spirit can allow the instruction of others to be absorbed into my heart and transform my life.

2. *Be still*

Stillness of heart relates to freedom from anxiety and an overactive mind. Far more than freedom from busyness, stillness is a condition of the heart and mind that are anchored securely in God, resting in Him. For the mind and heart to be still, I have to be living in the present, not worried about the past or the future. I learn to pray for a quiet heart.

3. *Be patient*

With my lists of goals for each day, each week, and each month, I like to know when I can expect a certain thing to be complete. I can't set a deadline on the work of the Spirit. The time table of God is different from my own. It might take Him years to accomplish what I want done in a day, or He may do a mighty work in a single moment that I thought would take years. Rather than rushing ahead of Him to accomplish what I think needs to be completed, I learn to look to Him for His timing.

I have found that the activity of the Spirit in my heart is imperative to spiritual productivity. With the direction, guidance, and voice of the Spirit, my religious endeavors are fruitless.

Life Application Questions

1. What is your understanding of the work of the Holy Spirit in your life?
2. Have you ever sensed His guidance and direction?
3. Pray that your heart would be open to the teaching and direction of the Holy Spirit.

CHAPTER 10

The Identity of the Called

The one who calls you is faithful and he will do it.

~ 1 Thessalonians 5:24

As I sorted through my own issues in search of God and His calling on my life, I noticed that many others seemed to be caught up with "the call." Some went to college with passion burning in their hearts to serve God. Some entered into ministry, thrilled that God would use them. Of those who entered ministry or missions, some lasted a lifetime, but others left "full-time service" after a couple of years.

Some—like me—who did not enter ministry directly after college, often spent time wondering about "God's will" for our lives. Sometimes college debt kept us from full-time service, or family issues or marriage to someone not "called" to the same area of service as we believed ourselves to be.

Deep inside many of our hearts, there resided the daily struggle that we tried to keep pressed down. Have we failed God? Have we copped out on the life God intended for us? The nagging insecurity of living outside the will of God was enough to keep my heart bound in daily despondency and at times drove me to become legalistic to overcome my sense of failure.

My Concept of "Calling"

As I grew up, I attended many Christian camps and other mission-focused services. Frequently, there was a call at the end of the service for people to dedicate their lives to Christian work. Many times I went forward. It was as though an intense force from within nudged me toward the front. At age eight, I committed my life to service the first time, and I believed without a doubt that I would be a missionary. My sense of calling was always based on the vows I made at these services.

As the years passed and this calling did not become a reality, I began to feel shame and guilt. Had I lied to God? I meant to keep those promises to serve Him, but it just didn't seem to work out. I knew God had a high value of covenants; what did He think of me for not keeping my word? How could He take me seriously in the future with my history of broken pledges?

With a sense of lost identity, I mused over these questions. What was my place in the body of Christ? Was I really called?

What AM I Called to Do?

Walt sensed that there was a great restless uncertainty in my soul about all this, and one day he asked me, "What are you called to do? If we believe that God put each of us on earth for a reason, that He gave us different gifts and abilities, to move forward you have to know what these are."

I knew that for years I had been struggling with this issue, yet as Walt said the words, I became aware of the root of my questions. I had boxed Christians into two categories: those who were called to Christian work full-time and those who were not. If I was not in full-time Christian work, I felt I had failed God. I did not believe the truth that God uses all people who are available to Him, and He created each of us to serve Him wherever we are.

The Parable of the Talents

I began to study Matthew 25:14–30. A master went on a long journey. Before he left, he entrusted three of his servants with talents. The first servant was given five talents, the second two talents, and the third one talent. When the master returned, he found that the first servant has invested his talents wisely and had doubled his talents, as did the second servant. However, the third servant was afraid and buried his talent in the ground so that he would not lose it. The master commended the first two servants who were diligent, but not the third who had lived in fear.

Matthew Henry's commentary[12] on this passage helped me to see numerous parallels in my life, and I learned three things about my calling or talents.

1. *Take account of what I am given.* Matthew Henry says that it is good to keep account of what we have received from the Lord in order to know what is expected of us. Mentally, I reviewed what I had received from the Lord: my husband, my children, my home, and my sewing business. These were all areas of responsibility that He had entrusted me with. My energy needed to be focused on faithfulness in these areas.

2. *I am entrusted with my own soul.* As Matthew Henry's commentary also mentions, God gives each of us the responsibility to care for our own soul, which includes the responsibility to renew my mind, battle strongholds, live according to biblical principles, and pray according to the promises of

12   Henry, Matthew. (2012). Bible Study Tools. (Jupiter Images Corporation) Retrieved June 14, 2012, from http://www.biblestudytools.com/commentaries/matthew-henry-complete/matthew/25.html?p=3 (all references to Matthew Henry in this chapter are from this site).

the Bible – doing all of these things relying on the power of God through His Spirit within me.

3. *The condition of my heart is of utmost importance.* It is easy for me to get caught up in how many talents I have versus those of someone else. When the day of accountability comes, we will be judged according to our faithfulness, not on our usefulness. The condition of our hearts will mark our faithfulness, not the greatness of our opportunities. Am I joyfully undertaking the tasks I have been given? Do I serve those under my care with love and compassion? This is the benchmark by which to examine my own heart.

Parallel to the Third Servant

As I continued to read Matthew Henry's commentary, I reached the part about the third servant. I had heard this passage all my life, though I never related myself to the third servant. As I read, I saw myself clearly. This third servant had two main issues that I had been working through.

1. *The servant came with assurance that his excuses for not investing would be accepted.* Looking at my circumstances, I tried to complain to God that I never went on to serve Him because I did not have the finances to complete Bible college. I thought that with the responsibilities of a family, I could do nothing for the Lord except try to be a good Christian, read my Bible daily, and go to church.

2. *The servant had an unfounded fear of the master (Matthew 25:24–25).* Henry comments that good thoughts of God would produce love that would make us diligent and faithful; but hard thoughts of God will produce fear that will make us apathetic and unfaithful. I recall the struggle I had with knowing God's will for my life and how I constantly waffled on decisions. It was all because I was afraid I was doing the

wrong thing, afraid I wouldn't follow the right path that He had for me. This amounted to doing nothing.

I had a false concept of God, believing He would be upset with me if I took a wrong step. I was in bondage to this fear of God because I did not know the love of God.

Biblical Examples of the Call

For the first time in my life, I began to objectively consider the issue of calling. The most practical way to do this was to look at biblical examples. Throughout the Scriptures, God called people—ordinary people—like you and me. But how?

Abram (later known as Abraham) was called directly by God (Genesis 12). God spoke to him with exact instructions. Abram was to leave his home town, friends, and relatives and travel to a place God would show him. God promised that He would make Abram a nation and that his lineage would be blessed.

Then there is the example of Moses. As he was tending to his sheep in the middle of the desert, a most peculiar thing caught his attention. A bush was aflame, but not burning up. As he walked over to examine the strange sight, God spoke to Moses, calling him to deliver the people of Israel out of Egypt (Exodus 3).

Looking at the account of these two patriarchs called by God, I noticed several things.

The Manner in Which They Were Called

I observed that both these Bible heroes were called by God in private. Abraham's call did not come in as dramatic a way as Moses'. Because of his personal relationship with God, Abraham did not question who was speaking to him; he knew it was God. For that reason, I believe that Abraham had spent time worshipping God, enough time that he was well acquainted with God's voice. The call of Moses was much more exciting but was equally private.

In both instances, I see that God directly chose those whom He ordained to fulfill His call, and the call took place between God and the called—without a third party present. I realized that I had been trying to understand my life's calling through inspirational speakers rather than seeking a message from God Himself.

The Instructions They were Given

I also noticed that at the time of the call, they did not receive all the instructions needed to implement their assignments. Instructions came one step at a time. Abraham was told that God would show him the land he was supposed to go to. In order to be shown, he first had to leave where he was. God did not lay out the travel map so that Abraham could plan a campsite for each night.

In the same way, Moses did not know the details of the Israelites' deliverance. He did not know about the ten plagues or crossing the Red Sea. He only knew that he was called to deliver the Israelites, that he would go before Pharaoh, and that God would be with him.

Both Moses and Abraham had a general idea of the long term plan (for Abraham, a new country and becoming a great nation; for Moses, deliverance of Israel from Egypt), but throughout their journey there had to be a complete reliance on God for direction. The Bible records several times when each of these men lost focus and fell into sin or unbelief. But they were called to service for a lifetime, and when they repented of their sin, God continued to use them.

I struggle with this step-by-step instruction, wanting to see the whole picture now. I have viewed service to God as a destination rather than a journey. God in His infinite wisdom knows that if I knew all that He will lead me to do in my lifetime, I would rush ahead of Him, trying to accomplish the work in my own strength.

What Commitments Had I Made?

If God really called me to mission work, was I living outside God's will by not being on the mission field? Had I gone forward because He had called me or because these were emotionally-charged services? As I reflected and prayed, the Lord showed me that in each instance, the Holy Spirit was nudging my heart, calling me to Himself. He planted in my heart this strong desire to draw closer in fellowship, but I had been so focused on finding out what my "mission" for God was that I had missed the fellowship.

God wasn't as concerned about the commitment of what I would do for Him but about a commitment to surrender to Him.

Does God Call All Christians?

I used to believe that only some people were called, but all Christians are called to a life of surrender as followers of Christ. God has a purpose for every believer in His plan. It is Christian service and requires obedience. Romans 12:1–2 says that we must present ourselves as a sacrifice to the Lord. Surrendering in purposeful obedience is this sacrifice as I allow Him to change my heart and cultivate a godly life within me.

Being a follower means that I don't know His plan. Surrender involves giving Him my dream of mission work and allowing Him to use me where He has placed me. I had my plans for mission work, much like I would approach a career. It was a goal set for myself that actually was an idol in my life.

This call to follow and to surrender is for everyone. Some may struggle with surrendering their time to the Lord, while others—like me—struggle more with the sins of the heart, which are unseen by those around us.

The Identity of a Follower

A major misconception in my sense of calling was that my identity was not in what I am but in what I did. Above all, as a

Christian, I am called to follow Christ. No matter what I do vocationally, following Him is most important; whether as missionary or as a layperson, I am simply a follower. He leads and I follow. I draw my direction from Christ, my head.

Being a follower is an identity. My responsibility is to be yielded, actively obeying and constantly listening. I must not find my value in the title writer, mother, wife, or missionary but simply in this—I belong to Him. What I am supposed to do as I follow is revealed to me only as I abide in Him.

Abraham and Moses were followers. God led and they followed. God fulfilled His purposes through them as they followed.

Freedom of Abiding

John 15 pictures a branch drawing all energy, nutrients, and life from the vine. The vine is the source of all. It is a continual process. Not for a moment can the branch survive on its own. It is 100% reliant on the vine. This is abiding: to rely on Him for all my strength. My flesh does not want to rely because it believes the lie that I am capable of something in my own strength, thinking I know a better way, an easier road, or a shortcut. Time and again I find my strength fails me when I wander off to try to serve Him on my own ability.

As I return to abide in Him, I find strength and power, which is my very source of life. I don't have to produce strength, struggle for peace, or lack power. It is all available to me if I abide in Him. However, when I find my soul anxious and weary, I know I have pulled away from abiding. This is the warning sign that I am not truly plugged into the vine. I seek Him until my soul finds quietness in His rest.

Direction from God comes when my soul is completely resting in Him. He may speak guidance to my heart through Scripture, circumstances, or a preacher, or it might be as I'm driving down the road fellowshipping with Him. No matter how or where, when the door of my heart is open as I abide in Him, He will speak, giving me the instruction I need to carry out His plans for me.

Following and abiding take the focus off of the tasks we think we should accomplish for God and put the focus on the step-by-step walk with God. Concentrating on what I can do for God leads me to believe that I am capable of doing something. This breeds an attitude of arrogance and self-sufficiency. However, when my attention is on abiding in Him, I recognize His rightful place, as He works through me. I am nothing without Him. Any work I accomplish is because He completed the work through me.

To rest in Him. To follow as He leads.

This is who I am called to be—a follower.

There is no other call.

Life Application Questions

1. Have you ever felt called by God?
2. What has God entrusted you with?
3. In what ways are you being faithful with the "talents" you have been given?
4. Pray that God would impress on your heart the call of a follower.

CHAPTER 11

To Guard My Heart

Above all else, guard your heart, for it is the wellspring of life.

~ Proverbs 4:23

What is spiritual warfare? My concept had been related to winning the lost or fighting the evils prevalent around me, standing for truth, and being a light in my community. However, in light of Matthew Henry's commentary on faithfulness in caring for one's own heart as the primary duty of believers, my perspective began to change.

I had been looking only at the battle outside of me and overlooking the battle within. My misconception had been that since I was saved, the battle for my heart was over. In truth, the enemy could not steal my eternal destiny, but he could steal my day-to-day fellowship with Christ when I was not actively guarding my heart.

Understanding the Heart

I could read Scripture and to the best of my ability apply it to my life. Through this, my actions conformed to the standards and belief of the Bible. Yet when I pondered my faith and the knowledge that I had of truth, it seemed more like rote memorization than the powerful Word of God that was alive in my heart. I had invested such efforts in learning the Bible. I knew it to be true; therefore, I did not fall into disillusionment. Instead, I focused on searching out the reasons for my lack of heartfelt belief.

Throughout the Bible, there are many references to the heart.

- Proverbs 4:23 – the warning to guard our hearts because all we do flows from it
- Mark 7:20–23 – from a person's heart comes evil
- 1 Samuel 16:7 – man looks at the outward appearance, but God looks at the heart

These few are enough to recognize the importance God puts on the heart.

The Book of Psalms also contains frequent references to the heart, often in the form of a prayer, asking God to search the heart as the writer acknowledges that only God can know the heart of man.[13] This is an example for me to follow. Only God can show me my heart. Only He can reveal to me the evil within. By my own efforts, I am unable to guard my heart or to make it pleasing to the Lord. In this, I must be wholly dependent on God. God desires that I know truth from my heart, but He is the only one who can teach me wisdom.[14]

Though I had dealt with my issues from the past, I began to comprehend that guarding my heart requires daily maintenance, like tending a garden. One day of neglected attention allows the weeds to grow. This is a sobering task, as my entire spiritual life flows from my heart.

The health of a person's eyes determines whether they live in blindness or have clear sight. In the same way, the eyes of my heart direct my inner man. The vision of my heart is given by the Spirit. When I choose to entertain wrong thinking, false speaking,

---

13   Psalm 7:9, 19:14, 26:2, 44:21, 139:2, 23
14   Psalm 51:6

or anxious pondering, I am choosing sight apart from the Spirit, the opposite of truth. The eyes of my heart do not gain spiritual sight by my own efforts but by fervently asking God on a continual basis to create in me a pure heart and to give me the eyes to see.

The Deceitfulness of the Heart

Due to the Fall of man, my inward bent is toward falsehood, whether it be outward actions of blatant lies, a slight twist in truth, or reliance on human effort. With ease I am deceived into thinking bad is good and good is bad. Without the vision of the Spirit, I am duped into believing all sorts of positive things about myself. I overlook my wrong motives, jealous attitudes, and complaining words because I am unaware of them. Only dependence on the Spirit uncovers the evils of our hearts, bringing humility as He shines light on my fleshly nature.

The Attack on the Heart

The enemy knows the heart's tendencies and is always eager to lead it astray. My concept of spiritual warfare was related to the evil acts of the unsaved people surrounding me. This distraction kept my attention away from my heart, where the enemy was wrecking havoc. I could perform the righteous actions of a professing Christian without doing them as unto the Lord.

God Is Holy and Jealous

Throughout Scripture, we see God as holy and jealous. As Deuteronomy 4:24 says, "The Lord your God is a consuming fire, a jealous God." He is jealous concerning receiving all the glory. He knows that if our focus is on Him, His purposes will be fulfilled, and we will experience the abundant life He desires for us. As a believer, my words, thoughts, actions, and beliefs need to be giving God the glory. This has little to do with the overt sins of lust, greed, and idolatry, and more to do with whether I am walking, speaking, and thinking according to truth.

Because of His jealousy, when I am dwelling in falsehood, He withdraws from fellowship. The opposite of truth is a lie; therefore, darkness. He does not dwell in darkness.

1 John 1:6 tells us that if we say we are fellowshipping with Him but live in darkness, we lie and are not living in truth. The crux of my darkness was that I had been living in many areas of untruth. I began to ask God to examine my heart for areas of deceit. These are some of the areas of falsehood that I had entertained in my own life, areas that I am learning to guard against through the strength and power of His Spirit.

1. The Thoughts I Think

My thoughts wander into worry and fear, easily projecting the "what-ifs" of tomorrow. There is a reason God told us not to worry about the future. He has already provided if I will seek to trust Him.

When anxious thoughts flood my mind, this is an opportunity to pray that Christ would take over my thoughts. I can ask Him to lead me to Scriptures of faith that I can proclaim and hold onto as the promise that He has already made a way. This is an occasion to enter into the battle for my heart. Entertaining false worry allows strongholds to grow in my heart, keeping me from the purity of trusting fellowship with my Savior.

The Bible so frequently speaks about our mind because having Christ-centered thoughts is the primary avenue to fellowship with Him.

2. The Words I Say

My spiritual life is affected by my words. My struggle is not with cursing but with complaining, faithless words. If I say something like, "I can't wait for this day to be over; it is too much for me," I am denying the power of God in my daily existence.

The words of my mouth should be an affirmation of my belief in God's strength, a strength that He has made available to all of us. When I feel unable, overwhelmed, or beyond myself, He is teaching me to pray, "Lord, give me strength for this day because I know I cannot do it on my own." This reflects the truth that only God is able and I am not.

When my words give way to proclaiming the stresses in my life without acknowledging that God has given me everything I need (most importantly His Spirit) to aid me in life, I am literally choosing to break fellowship with Him. Not only that, but my words come from my heart and reiterate to my heart my lack of faith. Speaking false words is a form of teaching my heart to distrust God.

It is not just what I speak concerning my trust in Him. What do I speak about other people? Speaking negatively of others means I do not trust that God is able to do a good work in them. When the words of my mouth dishonor God by complaining about good gifts He has given, or when I engage my mouth in words of worry, I am putting a voice to my fears, saying that they are bigger than the promises of God.

Every word out of my mouth has the ability to draw me closer to God or to distance me. My words testify whether my heart is focused on God or my earthly perception. With fresh fervor, I pray, "Lord, set a guard over my mouth."[15]

3. Treating the Bible as a Textbook

There is no other book that we study that is alive. All the study principles that we learn from grade school on up teach us how to learn from textbooks, which contain only words on a page. We learn so that we might grow knowledgeable in our field of study or in a hobby, etc.

---

15   Psalm 141:3

Though I longed for deep fellowship with God, my tendency was to fall into a routine of Bible study that produced knowledge. I thought studying the Bible was an avenue to knowing God. It taught me His character, love, and powerful works, but knowledge of the Bible does not equal fellowship with God.

There are so many wonderful exhortations in Scripture: to love our neighbor,[16] live at peace with all men,[17] pray always[18]. . . and the list goes on and on. All these are part of living for Christ, but I was tempted to believe that I could carry them out in my own strength, by my own resolve. If I take the Bible as a whole, I must believe that I can only carry out any command of Scripture through the power of His Spirit, for without Him, I can do nothing.[19] When I attempt to carry out my faith by my own efforts, I am actually living according to the flesh, denying the power of God, and entertaining the lie of self-sufficiency.

To guard against using the Bible as a self-help book, I realize my need to pray over each verse of Scripture that contains a command or exhortation, confessing to Him that I desire to follow the command and asking for His strength to do so.

4. Hindrances to Expectation

In Hebrews 11:6, we are told that it is impossible to please God without faith, that those who come to God must believe that He exists and that He rewards those who seek Him. This speaks of expectation. What do I believe about God and His power? Why was believing this such a struggle for me?

Over the years, I had embraced the teaching that God no longer works in the same way today that He did before the close of the canon of Scripture. As I wrestled with faith, trying to believe God

---

16   Matthew 22:36–40
17   Romans 12:18
18   1 Thessalonians 5:17
19   John 15:5

would fulfill His Word in my life, He began to show me that teaching created doubt in my heart, doubt that affected the following three areas:

- *God's Voice*: He desires to communicate with us through His Spirit that He placed within us. As I began to recognize the voice of the Spirit, I began to enjoy fellowship with Him.
- *God's Divine Orchestration and Intervention in my life*: I was unable to fathom that He did any work on earth beyond human means. I started to pray that He would show me the work that He does, and He did. Sometimes it is an orchestration of time, when I know that I could not accomplish my tasks in a given time, and yet with Him, it is done. At other times, He brings the very person I have been praying for across my path. Or I realize that He has divinely protected me from an accident. These are not coincidences, but God working on my behalf just as He promised.
- *God's Care of my Physical and Mental Well-being:* He is the great Physician. Scripture after Scripture talks about His healing power, yet I was unable to believe this. I had accepted every sickness as part of God's will for my life. I had even struggled to believe that He could heal my broken heart, thinking it was not His will till I reached heaven.

My expectancy in God had been dulled through glib "Christianese." Rather than rightly dividing what I read or heard, I believed well-meant, albeit false, teaching. I want to follow the example of the Bereans[20] and be continually examining Scripture, making sure that teaching I absorb is in line with the Bible. My goal is only to uphold the character and power of God.

---

20   Acts 17:10–11

5. Preoccupation with God's Will

The Bible teaches in Jeremiah 29:11 that God has a plan for our lives. But my excessive concern about God's will for my life was self-centered. I wanted to know what great purpose God had created me for without being aware that I was not carrying out His immediate will for me, which is to love God and love my neighbor. It was as if I expected Him to speak direction to me exactly at the time I asked. I was seeking the answer rather than seeking God. If every day I focus on bringing glory to God through repentance and faith, day by day He leads me. I don't know the future, but I don't need to.

How to Guard my Heart

Even though I began to understand the areas in which my heart was under attack, this knowledge did nothing for me unless it was applied. I have found the most practical way to fight this spiritual warfare is to pray Scripture. Jesus used this tactic when He was tempted by Satan during His forty days in the wilderness (Matthew 4:1–11). The entire Bible was given to reveal what God, who does not change, did in the past and what He will do in the future.

For every trial, for every situation, for every false thought or word, there is a promise and a truth in Scripture. Every exhortation to live a godly life is an opportunity to give myself to Him so that He can do His work in my heart to transform me into the image of His Son.

Until I began the practical application of entering into the battle for my heart, I had only head knowledge; my heart was far from Him. I knew the truths, but they were only intellectual facts. I tried to live my life in Christ by my own means, and my faith was dead, meaningless.

As He began to teach me the battle for my heart and reliance on His promises, the eyes of my heart began to open. My heart began to burn within me, quickened by His Spirit.

Life Application Questions

1. What did you learn about the heart?
2. What is your concept of the spiritual battle as related to guarding your heart?
3. Pray that God would help you to guard your heart.

CHAPTER 12

Hope Renewed

And we have the word of the prophets made more certain,
and you will do well to pay attention to it, as to a light shining in a dark place, until the day dawns and the morning
star rises in your hearts.

~ 2 Peter 1:19

What was this burning of my heart? It captivated me, filling my
empty places and flooding my heart with hope.

The Presence of Light

I believed that as a Christian, I should be a light in the world[21]
but had struggled with the darkness encasing my heart. Now I
know the light inside is His light because God is light.

Never before had I comprehended the truth of the spiritual
world of light and darkness. It was only an allegory that portrays
good and evil. As I experience the presence of light, I recognize how
great my darkness was. While my heart was filled with religious
attitudes, anger, fear, insecurity, and distrust, I was in darkness.

---

21   Matthew 5:14–16

The Transformation

Through the relationship of my heart resting in Him, a transformation took place and continues. As He burns away the flesh, the flame of God shines forth. I change. The world sees. I am a light in the world because His fire burns in my heart. This is not the burning of passion created by an altar call, dedicating my life to service, but the fire of the Living God, which changed my life in these areas.

- *The Fruit of the Spirit:* I longed for joy, peace, and victory. I did not have these because my heart was not drawing its supply of nutrients from the vine (John 15). A branch only bears fruit when it is in the vine. This speaks of deep communion beyond the external.

- A *Thankful Heart:* In this state of dependence, I am humbled to know that I can do nothing without Him; everything I am and do flows from Him. As I know this, thankfulness wells up in my heart. Until He gave my heart a revelation of my own unworthiness, I could not live in a state of thanksgiving. God is in proper perspective once again, and as John the Baptist said, "He must become greater; I must become less" (John 3:30).

A Testimony of God's Presence

The light within that transforms me also bears witness to the presence of the Holy Spirit. This is the deposit sealing my inheritance. It confirms to my heart every truth of the Bible, every promise of God, and I know that I know Him.

The promise of the Christian faith is the Living God. I knew the doctrine of His indwelling, yet I did not sense His presence in my heart, and I struggled with the reality of this truth. A favorite verse from childhood was God's promise in Hebrews 13:5 to never leave me. However, this truth affected me similarly to a calming bedtime fairy tale with a happy ending rather than the promise of the Almighty. Truth that was not impacting my life remained merely a story that did not affect how I lived. But as the truth of God's presence in my heart comes alive within, it propels me onward in the faith.

The Influence of His Presence on Fellowship

Our hearts were created with the desire for a relationship with God. Not just saved to be in heaven after this life, but with a craving to know Him in an intimate way during our lives here. Without knowing His presence, there is no fellowship. For me it was more like trying to build a relationship with an imaginary friend. I could talk all I wanted, and it was comforting to know that there was a friend I could speak to anytime I wanted, but it was not a two-way communication.

The Longing to Be With Him

True fellowship is a joy; I long to be with Him because my heart knows Him. It is not a duty of Christian responsibility, but He is the desire of my heart.

For years I was frustrated because I could not seem to reach Him. There had seemed to be this great chasm between us. I was striving to attain the relationship but never finding it. Now I have tasted of His rest as my heart hides under the shadow of His wing (Psalm 17:8), but many times I walk away, attempting to live by self-effort. This immediately breaks my heart from fellowship with Him, because I pulled away from the vine. Now that I have tasted of Him, I know what I am missing when I am not abiding in Him. It cultivates within me this great longing to be with Him all the time, now and forever.

The Focus of Hope

The focus of my hope had its basis in intellectual knowledge. I thought that being saved and knowing the right answers about Christ would have built the sure foundation on which to build my Christian life. I tried to logically build the foundation through the proper principles and disciplines but in vain. The focus of my hope had been on my own efforts, not on Him.

The very person of God, His character and His trinity – this alone can be the foundation on which to build life; the abiding Holy Spirit, without whom I am useless; the Father's love, which fills every crevice of my heart; the Son who died to set me free. My hope is in Him, that He would teach me to walk in His ways, giving me strength to yield to His Spirit, bestowing wisdom as I read His Word.

The Hope of Glory

Christ in me is my hope of glory.[22] How I puzzled over this! During the years of hopelessness, I believed that Christ was the answer but felt no hope of glory, no desire for heaven.

The reality of Christ in me as my hope has dawned on me slowly, and then all at once. It was as 2 Peter 1:19 says, the day dawned and the morning star arose in my heart. It was not by my own pursuit of knowledge but only as I sought Christ for Himself that He became the very presence of His glorious light shining forth in me.

Hope Renewed

My heart had been lonely, struggling to manifest the fruit of the Spirit, looking for peace. He drew me to Himself, put in my heart this longing that would not cease until I found Him to be all that He promised in Scripture. I sought Him till I found Him, until He burned in my heart. If the light of His flame grows dim,

---

22   Colossians 1:27

it bears witness that my heart has wandered. When this happens, I seek Him anew, pressing into His promises, asking Him to reveal the causes of my darkness, and praying for help to rest in His presence once more.

His fire burns in my heart with the desire that all might know the hope I have found in Christ. My emptiness has been satisfied by fellowship with Him. My darkness has disappeared as His light takes over. I am no longer content with intellectual knowledge but desire to have my heart continually filled with the knowledge of God. Herein hope is renewed.

I began with a desire to seek Him and find Him according to Jeremiah 29:13. Following this verse is another promise of what happens when we find Him: He will bring us back from captivity and back from the place where we had been exiled (Jeremiah 29:14). He brought me out of captivity, from darkness to light, out of bondage to freedom, to a place of sweet fellowship with Him. No longer is the promise just a future hope; now it is also a present reality. He did it for me, and He can do it for you!

Life Application Questions

1. What are your thoughts on Christ in you, your hope of glory from Colossians 1:27?
2. Do you sense the presence of God's light in your life?
3. Pray that He would teach your heart.

Lord, I want to seek You till I find You. I ask that You would make all the knowledge of Your Truth alive in my heart. I long to know You as my constant companion, as the Lover of my Soul and the Healer of my heart. I desire joy and peace, which are products of Your Spirit within me. Help me to yield in obedience, cooperating with Your work within so that You might produce fruit in my heart. I believe that You are able to complete a good work in me. Amen.

At the Foot of the Cross

At the foot of the cross

There is healing

At the foot of the cross

There is mercy

At the foot of the cross

Power flows from sinless blood

Love pours into broken hearts

From the perfect One

At the foot of the cross

Covered by His sacrifice

The Son of God sets me free

by Naomi Fata

Free printable bookmarks of this poem may be found online at: http://christianresourceministry.com/2013/09/24/ at-the-foot-of-the-cross-poem/

For more information about
Naomi Fata
&
Beyond Head Knowledge:
Knowing Christ Who Satisfies Our Hearts
please visit:

www.naomifata.com
naomi@christianresourceministry.com
@NaomiFata
www.facebook.com/AuthorNaomiFata

Ministry site which offers free printable cards and
bookmark poems by Naomi and other writers:
www.christianresourceministry.com
@CRMRhinebeck

For more information about
AMBASSADOR INTERNATIONAL
please visit:

www.ambassador-international.com
@AmbassadorIntl
www.facebook.com/AmbassadorIntl